HOW IT'S GONNA SUCK AND WHY

A Beginner's Guide to Teaching Abroad

Iain Thomas

For Hunter,
who, near as I can figure from third-hand sources,
enjoyed this book

CONTENTS

INTRODUCTION

Stumbling & Bungling

Have you ever come off a 2-hour bus ride at 7:00am to an awards ceremony in an imposingly elegant hotel, sniffing off the onset of a cold, been given an ice cream-like ball of guacamole, a tiny cup of coffee and been left to listen to a telemarketer comparing the sales department to Gandhi? If not, I don't recommend it. It's not pleasant.

Looking back, I'm ashamed at myself for not being more grateful, but the whole thing kind of blindsided me. I was given an excellence award for a class that was mediocre at best. I remember it well because it was the first time my coordinator observed me. It was the first time I had *ever* been observed, in fact.

I'd been my own harshest critic up till then. I existed in a perpetual state of fear that I was doing the job wrong and thought it was only a matter of time until my bosses caught on and fired me. The class in question was so unremarkable that I can hardly remember what happened—there was a PowerPoint about a bear. I *do* remember that much. (Personally, I'm pleased that you had a bear in your lesson. I never could figure out how to put a bear in one of mine)

What I remember even more, though, is the apprehension I had for my feedback. I was sure I'd get raked over the coals, that my coordinator would shout "a bear? Seriously!? What kinda circus do you think we're running?" But, no. Everything was just fine. Nothing was on fire; I communicated well with the students and even made jokes. Everything was apparently just fine.

But in what world did "just fine" equate to an award? I felt almost embarrassed to receive it, like at any moment one of the well-dressed people across the room would leap onto the table and call me out as an impostor. The only credential I had going for me was a CELTA—a certificate from a month-long training I took after college which I swear they only gave me out of pity. Throughout the course I was a disaster: I never made it through my entire lesson plan in time, I gave the students materials which were way too hard for them, and—to top it off—I was voted "most likely to offend someone" because I had accidentally called someone ugly. (And they were right on the money: I made a woman cry on my very first day of work).

Yet there I was—tired, sniffling, and taking my teaching award. I would get that same award two more times, if you can believe that. You could take that as evidence of me being a "good teacher," but I wouldn't venture to say that. And I don't say so out of modesty.

Teaching is a crapshoot. That's what I've come to realize. I could spend my entire life teaching in every imaginable country, with every possible level of student, and everything could still go wrong in the classroom. That's not to say there aren't good teaching methods, of course, but to focus solely on that belies the volatility of the profession.

If I've gotten anywhere in my time teaching, it's only been through stumbling and bungling, and stumbling and bungling is precisely what I'll keep doing for as long as I'm in this field.

Even so, how do you package that as advice? Would it be enough for me to tell you that you're going to screw everything up?

Yeah. If I was in the business of bumper stickers then "you're gonna screw it all up" would be a top-notch piece of wisdom to dispense. I'm far too long-winded for that, though, so here: have a book. In the following pages I've done my best to summarize five years of stumbling and bungling into a digestible (hopefully helpful) format. In a profession where we're all idiots, it's my hope that my idiocy will make you a little less of one.

Enjoy.

LIVING ABROAD

Why do it?

It's a fair question, y'know? Why leave behind friends, family, security, (your *home*) just to spend a year living in a place where (spoiler warning), you'll be forgotten by the time the next guy swoops in?

Each week you'll spend more time preparing for everyday life than actually *seeing* the country you're in, than actually *giving* the classes you were hired for. If you don't already know the language, every interaction will become an embarrassing struggle to do something even as simple as buying floss (I don't know why, but this was exceptionally hard to find in Japan). And don't start thinking that every interaction with students will be a meaningful cross-cultural exchange either. Groups of apathetic teens and kids far outnumber those of adults looking to rub shoulders with foreigners; what's more, even adults are susceptible to being demanding or just plain boring.

I mean, it's exotic and all, but you get sick of it pretty quick. Before you get into this job, you owe it to yourself to honestly answer the big question: why do it? Otherwise, you can end up in a real depressing place with your life.

In my case, teaching has always been a means to an end. It's not unpleasant, but teaching, *teaching* has never been my cup of tea. If you, on the hand, are just gung-ho about teaching itself, if that ranks #1 on your list, then feel free to skip this section 'cause you've probably already got it all figured out. Or, if you're just here for schadenfreude, feel free to keep reading.

I went to Japan out of a vague, half-hearted need to justify my anthropology degree by living abroad. Problem 1: I wasn't really into anthropology; I thought the whole quasi-philosophical cultural trivia aspect of it was cool, but at no point did I want to *be* an anthropologist. I'd just followed the path of least resistance and going to Japan was very much the same. I was driven by a mixture of guilt and the hazy idea that at some point I'd man up and take charge of my life.

Just try explaining *that* to a student with limited language abilities. Beyond making the inevitable conversation of "What's your hobby? Do you prefer dogs or cats?" or "why did you come to Japan?" unbearably awkward, it cast a cloud of uncertainty over the job itself. A pro would've snapped back with a self-assured "I came for the sushi! Ha ha ha!" But I was anything but that. I took that question all too seriously because not even I could answer it. My first year of teaching was a fumbling cringefest.

Case in point: I messed up *learning* the *names* of my students; for the longest time, I engaged in awkward acrobatics to avoid revealing it, hoping to catch one of their classmates saying it so I could hide my own humiliating gaffe. I won't even go into what the usual classes (or lack thereof) were like because that's material for another dozen sections.

My time in Mexico was more goal-oriented. I came to polish my Spanish, to be with my future wife, and that's precisely what I did. I had gained some basic teaching abilities at the expense of my Japanese students, but even without those I probably would've been okay. Why? Because when you know where you stand, you know where you can go.

But that's just the teaching side of things. There's no denying that the TEFL industry wouldn't exist if not for the sexy tourism side of it. If this is what you're gunning for, then rest assured: you're in good hands. Pretty much any job you apply for will include this in some form. The extreme examples are job advertisements riddled with stars and exclamation marks which shout "15 MINUTE WALK FROM THE BEACH" or "COME EXPERIENCE THE REAL THAILAND." I can't speak to how legit these are, but knock yourself out if you want to apply for them, just don't disparage job offers without beaches and margaritas.

Even the most modest and unassuming job will come with a bit of tourism attached. In Japan, for example, my boss made a point of showing me around town on my first day and several times throughout the year took me out for dinner. In Russia, our administrator took us on weekend excursions to churches and abandoned mansions off the beaten path. Finally, there are the students: a lot of them will be itching to show you the local sites and will even insist on paying for your transport and meals.

Whether you're driven by a love of teaching or just wanderlust, you can find fulfillment in this field. Just make sure you know what exactly it is that drives you.

There are some sketchy schools out there

My first job in Mexico was one I found through Craig's List next to an advertisement promising to teach you English in a week through hypnosis. I knew nothing about the poster other than what the job details said and what his Linkedin profile said: that he was a freelance recruitment specialist. I couldn't even find his "school" through Google.

If you think everything I'm describing here sounds highly suspect, then you're right—it is. If you find it laughable that someone would follow up on such a job posting, then you're right—it is. Have a laugh at my expense because that's exactly what I did.

At the time, I was desperate to live in the same country as my future wife, but finding a job near her was tricky. A lot of the postings for Latin America one finds online will be for volunteer gigs ("come experience the beautiful beaches of Guatemala!" "Make a difference in the tiny villages of the Sierra Norte!"). What's more, it's undeniable that a school will be more willing to hire someone who's already in the country than someone who promises to come down in three or four months. It's just logistically simpler.

Needing a job that would support me financially and put me relatively close to Mexico City, my options seemed slim, so I took what I could get.

What followed was less of a job and more of a weird homestay experience. As it turned out, the school wasn't so much a *school* as a *dining room* in my boss's house. I arrived for the "grand opening" of the school and, lacking any students to teach, they put me to work on spreading the word. This basically entailed doing odd jobs with my boss's family: hanging a giant banner outside their house; accompanying the grandfather through suburban neighborhoods to stick pamphlets into people's mailslots; harassing passersby in supermarket parking lots to tell them about how they could learn English from a real-live foreigner (me!)—stuff like that.

Mind you, none of this I say to speak badly of my hosts. On the contrary, I was taken in with great hospitality. I was included in the family meals and accommodations were arranged for me in a nearby jumble of apartments; I didn't even mind that there was a cow next door or that the room was little more than a concrete box with a bed and shower; it was livable enough for me. My boss and his family were nothing but cordial to me from beginning to end. Moreover, I felt lucky to be practicing my Spanish in household conversations with real people. They were simply a normal family trying to establish a new business. The issue wasn't that; it was more with the job itself.

My duties weren't just restricted to teaching; I was also supposed to be a telemarketing headhunter. Each afternoon, I was expected to make cold calls to companies from a Skype number officially registered as being in Los Angeles. This consisted of me pulling up a massive Excel document full of company numbers fetched from the internet and plugging through them one by one. "Secretaries exist only to be obstructionists," my boss quipped, and our goal was to bypass them so as to talk with the real decision-makers. We found the names of the companies' CEOs online and tried our best to sound casual when we asked to speak to them. If we succeeded, it would give us a brief moment to pitch our headhunting services to the annoyed moguls of startups across the States. If we landed the pitch perfectly, they'd theoretically turn to us for recruitment services. About 98% of the time, though, we got hung up on.

It was incredibly stressful. Even so, I convinced myself that teaching would be more my speed and that the cold calls would become nothing more than a brief, unpleasant chore. Such hopes were totally dashed by the time I had my first class.

When I asked what the school's methodology was, rather than an explanation I was handed a hefty book of grammar exercises. The philosophy of the school was something I would describe as "sweatshop English." There was no curriculum, just a series of text-dense exercise books and a rough weekly plan of doing writing on Monday, free-speaking on Friday, and grammar everywhere else. Students were deposited around the table and made to work through the book until their hour was up. Meanwhile, the "teacher's" job was to circle the group for errors like a lion in search of sluggish gazelles. If an explanation was needed, it was given in rapid-fire Spanglish. Anyone who couldn't keep up was scolded for slacking off. Aside, maybe, from the writing and free conversation day, no effort was made to personalize the language at all.

A school is one of the easiest businesses to open. Whether it's a guy posting flyers on a telephone pole or a dodgy office on the top-floor of a vegetable shop, anyone who claims to understand English can claim to teach it. The quality of the service isn't as apparent as with, say, a clinic or a restaurant. If we get sick after eating contaminated meat from a restaurant, we know not to eat there anymore. If a clinic performs sham surgeries or liberally writes prescriptions for opioids, it'll be shut down by the authorities. It's not so easy with a school.

Take the first place I worked at in Japan. We may have played loose and fast with the conversation classes for adults, but it didn't matter since adults are competent enough to take charge of their own learning. What did matter was trying to apply the same strategy to kids' classes. Children were grudgingly accepted by the school as a necessary economic evil; to prosper as a business, we had to adapt to the market and there were simply more children who needed to learn English than adults (as is the case anywhere). We were given textbooks and plenty of materials were available in the office, but there was little to no oversight of what we actually *did* in the class.

What I *actually did* was a lousy job. I won't deny that. I had no idea how to teach children, so my classes often devolved into forcing them to work from their textbooks for the 45 minutes we were together. This was my first experience with the sweatshop English model, and though it was clear to me from the start that it was harmful, I was clueless about how to teach differently. I made half-hearted attempts at using games, fumbled about with flashcards, made needlessly complicated handouts, tried singing the robotic songs from the book, tried acting out the dialogues from the book, but was only greeted with blank stares. The embarrassing thing wasn't so much my failure as a teacher, though, as the fact that I was allowed to continue doing it.

I wasn't the only one, either. My colleague gradually got so sick of the job that he didn't even plan his lessons. He just ran dozens of copies of whatever children's book from the library struck his fancy and read it out loud for the class. To this day I can still vividly recall hearing his cheerless voice through the wall reading the *Cat in the Hat* as one would've read a blender instruction manual.

Suppose one of those children had complained to their parents. Suppose they had said "today my teacher did nothing but read me a book" or "today we just did grammar exercises." From the perspective of a parent—especially a parent who was schooled along those same lines themselves—how would it ever become clear that there was a problem? The damage isn't fully seen until years later when past students with their heads full of conjugation tables and droning recitations of Dr. Seuss attempt to interact with the language for the first time and realize they can't. Even then, chances are they'll chalk it up to just not having the knack for language, or to just not having studied hard enough because—honestly—who can understand what effective teaching is unless they've been lucky enough to receive it?

I left that school in Mexico after the very first class. I couldn't subject myself—or, more importantly others—to the drudgery of sweatshop English. Luckily, I got picked up by another school shortly thereafter, one with classrooms, administrative oversight, standardized tests, textbooks, study plans—the works—and I was happy there for the next two years.

That's not to say that a small school can't cut it, though. A school in your mom's basement or classes through Skype can be run just as well as a big-name chain like Berlitz or International House, but what really makes the difference is the guiding vision. All too often the people who establish schools are only in it for the money; they've never taught themselves, but they feel their background in marketing, international relations, tourism, or "insert whatever field here" gives them the expertise to decide how others should be taught.

After Mexico, I had a variety of options for where to go next and I resorted to the same method I've used for all my other jobs (sans my adventure through Craig's List). In the early days TEFL was a backpacker's gig. Like Leonardo DiCaprio out of *The Beach*, you just touched down in a bizarrely exotic land with nothing but your luggage, burned through all your cash, and then drifted towards the only thing you had any competency in—English. In some ways it's still like this, but reputable schools will at least screen out vagabonds who only want the job to keep themselves in booze and prostitutes.

If shoestring globe-trotting isn't your thing, though, then the jobs board of Dave's ESL Café is your best bet. New offers roll in every day, so your only limitation (aside from, y'know, qualifications) is how squeamish you are about where to go. Find an offer you like, send your email with the requested documents, go through a Skype interview without making yourself out to be a bumbling idiot and—bam—you're in.

That's how I found my last job. I went combing through ads of schools clamoring about access to tropical paradises or about how much money potential teachers would make. One representative of a school in China even told me—not lying here —"just don't come into work drunk and you'll be fine." That, alongside his stories of teachers visiting bars every day and night, coming into work hungover made it an obvious no.

There were lots of attractive offers, but what I chose for my final teaching job was an unassuming little school in Moscow. They made no great claims to fame, but they did something which was unprecedented for me: they set aside a fourth of a teacher's working hours for planning lessons. That preparation time represents a significant chunk of a teacher's job and one that goes unrecognized because it doesn't translate into any clear profit. (Any teacher will gripe endlessly about that if you get them started). From the moment I saw that, I knew I would be in good hands. I knew that the rules of the school would be guided from a teaching perspective, not a business one. Sure enough, it was a good place to work.

Principles like paying for planning time ought to be the rule, not the exception, but they won't be. For every school out there that respects its teachers, there are at least five more that just hire them to be sweatshop managers. Don't fall into that trap.

"Culture" is what you make of it

It was a Sunday night at the Hard Rock Café in late winter. After having stupidly wandered around for an hour in the howling wind with only a fleece jacket, I felt I was coming down with something. It was late, I was tired, an hour-long train ride separated me from home and I had to work the next day. In spite of all that, I'd decided to come to the weekly language exchange.

And it was worth it. Here I was nursing a beer with rapt attention as the guy next to me recounted his crackpot odyssey across Russia. People came up to our table and tried to elbow into the conversation, but I wasn't having it. No one was gonna interrupt the Hollywoodesque story I was listening to.

Through halting English this guy told me about train-hopping through the country with nothing more than a guitar and a sleeping bag. He paid his way with whatever paltry amounts he could scrounge up from busking, camped out in fields under the stars each night (and by some miracle it never rained). He arrived at Vladivostok—on the edge of the world—determined to cross the Pacific in a sailboat to Boston (yes, I know it's on the opposite coast, I'm just repeating what I was told). If he pulled it off, he could write a book about the experience which everyone would read and then, as he figured, the money would start rolling in.

But it didn't work out so well. After buying a boat, he set off just in time for a storm to chuck it against a rock. He got stranded on a tiny island, haggled with the islanders to take him back to the city, started saving up for another boat, met a Christian missionary from Montana who got deported, and then—at some unclear point—decided he would instead travel back to Moscow, learn German, and then apply for German citizenship.

In some capacity this person was probably crazy. Heck, his story probably wasn't even true. He was hardly the kind of character you see advertised in tourism pamphlets, but if he wasn't the "IT" thing that living abroad is supposed to give you, then what was he?

That whole "IT" thing of visiting exotic places has always rubbed me the wrong way. I mean, what? Is the word "culture" supposed to be a magic invocation which will summon up tribes of brightly dressed African children who'll dance with you in ceremonial rites at the snap of your fingers? 'Cause people certainly treat it that way.

Maybe I'm just a wet blanket, but as a *cultural*-flipping-*anthropologist,* I feel professionally justified in saying it's a junk word. With as much as every new generation of anthropologists has rebranded it, it's become a catch-all for "this doesn't fit anywhere else, but I guess it's important."

That allows it to be pretty much whatever you want it to be. Observe:

> Inspirational quote on the cap of a Snapple bottle?—clearly put there because of our cultural need to find meaning through consumption of material goods.

Stubbed your toe?—if not for the absence of highly rhythmic dance in our Anglican heritage you would've deftly leapt aside. Instead, you belong to the stubbed toes culture.

I would gladly keep throwing flippant examples at you, but that'd just annoy you. You'll tell yourself "well, clearly this guy doesn't have anything of value to offer but complaints. What's his point, anyway?" To which I say, "yes, I'm annoying. Bear with me, though, because I do have a point."

Thanks to a dead Chinese guy, I've come to think of culture like this: it's a goblet word. In the *Zhuangzi*, Chuang Tzu talks about how there are words which are essentially "no-words." Just like a goblet is an empty vessel, a no-word takes whatever you pour into it. In Burton Watson's translation, he puts it like this: "with words that are no-words, you may speak all your life long and you will never have said anything. Or you may go through your whole life without speaking them, in which case you will never have stopped speaking." In essence, goblet words do everything and nothing at the same time. They're empty, and that's precisely what makes them useful.

If you ask people why they choose to teach abroad, a lot of them will cite "culture" as their main reason. That's what my very first ever colleague in Japan said. He had already taught in Thailand and South Korea for a few years and it seemed that Japan was just another notch in his belt. The guy was fit to conquer the world—and I mean, literally, he was *fit*.

For our profiles on the school website, he wrote that he was dedicated to developing his body and mind to their maximum potential. To that end he worked out every day and religiously stuck to a strict diet. This guy's muscles practically exploded out of every shirt he wore. He joined a martial arts club in our city and apparently really wowed his sensei. He was a force to be reckoned with; I dreaded the possibility of ever getting on his bad side.

And that's what made it all the more puzzling when he broke down. It was a gradual thing: it started out with him getting more and more irritated with me. Frankly, I don't blame, though, because I *am* annoying. On shadowing his first class, I jumped at the chance to explain the word "aunt" to a student by drawing a family tree on the board—something he later described as me saying "I'm the man here, not you. I don't care if it's your class. I'mma cut in anyway." The first time we went out for a walk together I also joked about aloe vera's vast healing potentials being a wive's tale (which, for some reason, he took offense to).

We eventually made up, though, and kept our respective distances. I figured that was that, but no.

After that, he started picking up strange habits. He failed to pay for his gas and electricity bills, so our boss had to call the companies and pay extra for them to be reactivated. He was hardly dissuaded by the inconvenience he'd caused, though, as he did it again the next month. And again. On top of that, he started eating canned fish in the classroom and leaving the tins despite multiple complaints about the smell. He stopped planning his classes and just opted to read out loud from the book. For kids' classes, he would arrive a few minutes before the class, pull a children's book at random from the shelf, and brazenly make a dead sequoia's worth of copies as our boss looked on in impotently polite horror. Fish-can-man had a Master's degree in education, so I guess a lot of us just rolled with it. We figured he was the expert.

But the students begged to differ. A lot of them complained about him or bailed on us altogether. He seemed disinterested in their lives. Instead of initiating conversations or helping them along with questions, he just hunkered down and glared at them from across the table. This all climaxed on his final day. After getting his final paycheck, he just jetted. Poof. He didn't even show up for his final classes. No notice, no note, no nothing.

We needed to get the keys to his apartment, but we had no idea where they were. My boss had driven by his place and seen the lights on, but she was too afraid of him to go up and ask. So, by virtue of us living in the same complex, that responsibility fell to me.

I returned home only to be greeted by a bread crumb trail of trash bags scattered around the main stairway. The Japanese are pretty strict about sorting their garbage. There's a specific day for clothes, electronic devices, paper, and so on; put the wrong thing out on the wrong day and you'll get fined for it. That clearly wasn't a concern for him, though, as he'd dumped all his garbage into mixed bags and tossed them everywhere. Sidestepping the remnants of his years with us, I ascended to his floor and steeled myself before knocking on the door, expecting to be clobbered for having disturbed him.

But the door gave on my first knock. It was unlocked. The apartment was dark, the key on the table, and my ex-colleague, long gone.

A few days later he posted an update on Facebook. It was a picture of him triumphantly holding up his Japanese visa card which now had a hole punched in it. The caption read "goodbye Japan." The secretary hired a special guy to help her clean out the apartment, which had further mountains upon mountains of rubbish waiting inside. I got assigned his leftover classes, and that was that.

I never found out what happened to him and I probably never will. There was a girlfriend he had left in South Korea—she may have had something to do with it—or maybe it was just the working conditions. My boss once remarked that he was more accustomed to big city life since that's where he'd worked in Korea before. I think she hit the nail on the head there, but didn't it run counter to his character? Wasn't he supposed to be "in it for the culture?"

If so, then the culture of our little city had been too much for him. And, frankly, that wouldn't surprise me. Our culture—to the extent of it being experiences and events—often boiled down to weekend excursions with old people. There was no shortage of retired, bored housewives who wanted to invite us out.

I played along with it. I went to piano concerts, talent shows, flamenco exhibitions, art fairs in the street, tiny towns which were known for little else than pottery or noodles cooked on a shingle, caves, plateaus, mountains, forests, or simply to people's houses for lunch. And—yeah—maybe my company was a little dull and the conversation was strained for lack of their English abilities, but wasn't it all culture? Like, bona fide, real-deal culture with the actual people?

Prior to his breakdown, I'd actually gone *with* my colleague on one of these excursions. His student had been hounding him for an outing and after burning through all his excuses, Fish-can-man finally caved. He brought me along as a kind of human buffer with no more explanation than "he has an island he wants us to visit."

What I had in mind was a James Bond type villain, and the dude's background did little to dispel that image. He was a wonder. We never learned his real name as he—and everyone at the school—referred to him as John Doe. Not at all conspicuous on the school register—John Doe—there amongst a sea of Tanakas, Yamadas, and Yokos. Even so, the staff never thought twice about it.

The island in question was Tsunoshima. (If you've got a second, look it up; it's gorgeous). As it turned out, he didn't *own* the island but rather had grown up there. Near as I can figure, he wanted someone to listen to his nostalgizing, which wasn't disagreeable at all. We went to the beach where he used to go fishing as a child. We had lunch together at a quaint little restaurant. He recounted how the island had changed, how trees had grown and been cut down, how the bridge to the mainland had changed things. We climbed to the lighthouse where we found a plaque dedicated to friendship between the US and Japan alongside an oak tree which, surprisingly, his father had helped to plant. We went to his summer house for a beer and, as dusk fell, he suddenly seemed deeply sad. All this, and he never told us his real name.

Surely that was culture. Even I would call it culture. For Fish-can-man, though, I guess it was just an inconvenience. He regularly dodged these outings, even going so far as to abandon his own farewell party. That day when he skipped town, his students were left waiting a full hour for him—alone in an empty classroom surrounded by balloons and gifts.

I'm making him out to be a first-class jerk here, but his frustration was nothing unusual. There comes a point in teaching abroad—call it culture shock, if you want—where everything becomes just one frustration after another. You go to the supermarket and wind up buying detergent instead of chocolate milk mix because you couldn't read the label; you get stranded at the train station overnight because you misunderstood the attendant's instructions; you don't make any friends; you feel this yawning abyss of difference between yourself and your colleagues and students. Your students, in fact, become a singular sore point for you because they are what they are. Their manual for life just doesn't match up with yours and probably never will.

And chalk it all up to culture, if you want. If your students like or don't like games, maybe it's because their socioeconomic status and historical oppression by neighboring countries inevitably made it that way. God knows I've attributed my Japanese students' passivity to the oppression of the closed country period where samurai, I'm told, simply rode around towns chopping rude people's heads off. I can't prove that—probably no one can—but it's a convenient place to put the blame. The meaning of what happens abroad—or even at home, if you want—becomes whatever vessel you choose to put it into.

But the contents are the same either way. Keep that in mind if your reason for going abroad is the "IT" thing of culture. That category of exoticism is however big you choose to make it. Set it too narrow and don't be surprised if you walk away with nothing but disappointment.

The human element

There was a time in Mexico when I occasionally got rented out for teaching workshops, both in and out of the school.

For one, I got a lift to a girls' school in a far-flung area of the city I'd never visited. It wasn't long after a major earthquake had hit and they were still having some infrastructure problems. There was no Wi-Fi for the activities I had planned, the bulb in the projector from our first classroom burned out, and they were having problems with the electricity. Even so, it all worked out pretty well. We talked about implementing deductive and inductive grammar approaches in the classroom, swapped stories, and just enjoyed each other's company in general.

I wound up carpooling back home with one of the other teachers and we really hit it off. She told me about her life: about working in a national park in the states, about marrying a foreigner, coming to work in Mexico, raising a family, and—above all—about teaching. That day she told me something that really stuck with me. She said that no other job, except maybe being a priest, gave you access to the personal lives of people like teaching did. No other job would give you the same sample of people's interests, routines, families, hopes, fears, quirks—what-have-you. She liked it for that.

And I agree. If TEFL is just a chance to familiarize yourself with a foreign country, then the teaching aspect is probably the best way to do it. Forget about sight-seeing or local history, you get to meet the *actual people*—uncensored, unfiltered, totally candid (often to the point of being annoying).

Your students let you into their lives, even their homes, making you almost a member of the family. I worked with an older woman in Japan, for example, who on occasion would bring me cooked meals in the school. We went sight-seeing. She sent me holiday cards. She even invited me over to her house a few times.

When Christmas rolled around, she asked me to drop by her

house and see her decorations; so, I went wandering through the cold, dark streets of the city one weekend night and suddenly came upon it: this gaudy display of wattage with an animated Santa Claus climbing up onto the roof and colored bulbs splattered across every soffit and wall imaginable. It was illuminated to the point of making her house look like it was on fire; I guess that's why it all felt so warming. There were Christmas decorations all around the city, sure, but hers was the only house in the residential area to have lights: for blocks and blocks, everything else was just bland and commonplace.

We—she, her husband and I—sat down for dinner together. She played the piano, demoing a piece she was working on for an upcoming competition. I saw her Hanamatsuri display of little dolls. They taught me a new idiom in Japanese. We looked up my parent's house in Google Street View. I have a photo from that night which captures the feeling perfectly: the two of us are sitting on the couch, chatting in low tones; I'm hunched over with my horrible glasses sitting crooked on my face, she's wearing a faded sweater, and in the foreground there's a coffee table with an array of ceramic Santa Clauses. She collected those things. Of all things to collect—ceramic Santa Clauses—who'd've imagined it?

I ask you: what other job gives you that kind of connection with your clients (or students—if either word fits at this point)?

Then again, being privy to personal details doesn't always make you a family member. Sometimes you get recast as a personal therapist instead.

When I said I made a woman cry on my first day of work, I wasn't exaggerating (well, *a little* maybe, as it was actually my second). That day we were doing a listening per the instructions of my predecessor—who had done *exactly the same* listenings from *exactly the same* website—and despite my assurances that we would listen again, one of the women was so overwhelmed that she burst into tears. "They talk so fast," she sobbed through her hands. Without much recourse left, I scrapped the listening and went to comfort her: "hey, it's okay. Don't worry. We don't have to do the listening. Let's just talk."

Little wonder, that class was always super tense. In the end, I just drew pictures on the board according to whatever the conversation was: bees?—let's draw a hive and talk about related vocab. Snakes?—let's talk about types and what to do if you get bit by a venomous one; this is what a rattlesnake looks like, these are called fangs.

It all became a weird weekly-classroom-tea-party-Pictionary thing. A lot of the women loved baking and every week would bring a cake or a plate of brownies. They were delicious—don't get me wrong—but try enjoying a pastry while a whole room of expectant eyes are glued to you in silence and you're thinking "snap. I need to get the ball rolling because no one's talking." You choke down the chocolate frosting, cough out a question about Yuko's weekend, and meticulously alternate between eating and listening so that no one feels neglected.

There was an element of group therapy to it too. As with all my classes, the issue of "my such-and-such-relative died last week" wasn't uncommon; medical problems came up; there was a weird day when we talked about a boy who got struck by lightning while playing baseball; but, true urbanites that they were, the one that resonated best with everyone was pets. I dunno how or why we got on the topic of euthanasia (you see? you see why my CELTA teachers dubbed me "most likely to offend someone?") but I just rolled with it. I taught them words like "injection" and "put down" and everyone entered into sad reminiscence mode. Oddly enough, it's probably the best class I had with them—maybe because I could relate to it. It was encouraging—reassuring even—to know that these folks on the other side of the world loved their dogs just as much as I loved the one I had lost that same summer.

Any why not? Empathy enriches the job. There were other students in Japan who I simply couldn't get to be open with me. One—a mother who I did a terrible job preparing for the TOEFL —even brought her son to class a few times. You'd think that'd make us instant besties, but there was always an uncomfortable distance between us. She would sometimes tell me how difficult her job was, how challenging it was to raise her kid, but all in a very matter-of-fact way. Simply put, she never complained. No matter how much I encouraged her to reflect with an "oh, that sounds hard" or "and how did you feel?" she just told me "it can't be helped."

Classically Japanese, and very American of me to think that people want to express themselves, I guess. You can't really blame me, though: the most this woman had to offer in the way of conversation was an anecdote about going to a newly opened Starbucks, waiting in a massive line for an hour, then deciding it wasn't worth it and going back home. She was the type of person who would tell you "I've been to Paris" and after a comedic pause would add "I had a layover there! Ha ha ha ha." She even *wrote* "ha ha ha ha" in her diary at things which were most definitely not amusing in the least. She could've benefited from complaining. Our *class,* which was supposed to be *dedicated* to conversation, would've benefited from complaining.

Rapport building isn't just a buzz word. It improves a class. It improves *the job.* To build rapport, though, you have to make the classroom a safe place, you have to earn people's trust and that means sometimes you have to be a shoulder to cry on. Ever heard of the *ikemeso danshi*? They're hot Japanese dudes that women hire to make them cry. Teaching's not so far removed from that, especially with emotionally fragile housewives. You put yourself out there and hope for the best.

And it's *exhausting.* It's exhausting when it does work and even more when it doesn't. In Mexico, Saturday used to be my busiest day. I taught ten hours straight—one 5½-hour class in the morning and one 4-hour class immediately after. For one block of courses I found myself in the weird situation of having one highly reciprocal class and one totally unparticipative one. The first was complete asshattery as every activity devolved into jokes and anecdotes—fun, but stressful to deal with when you're supposed to be the one responsible for putting everyone back on track. The second was a group of three totally different students: a Mormon teenager, an aloof sociology student, and an imagination deprived woman whose only joy in life was shoes. Every conversation in the book went pretty much like this:

Me: What's your favorite movie?

Sociology student: ...

Mormon teenager: I like the new [INSERT POPULAR MOVIE HERE]

Imagination deprived woman: I think that movie's stupid. I don't understand why people watch movies at all. Why watch something that's not even real? Dogs can't talk and they never will.

She *literally* asked that once: "why watch movies if they're not about real things?" We were working with a speaking heavy textbook, yet every conversation nosedived as soon as Mrs. I-have-no-joy-in-my-life-to-speak-of opened her mouth. Each conversation lasted about 2 minutes tops. Try filling four hours with that. At certain points I was so exasperated that all I could do was start laughing while yanking on my hair in frustration.

The human element of teaching is my least favorite part of the job; ironically, it's also the most rewarding. I'd have no material—neither complaints nor interesting stories—for this book if not for my students and the odd cast of characters I've met along the way. A peaceful variant of the job would involve nothing but planning the lesson, dispensing materials, and grading them once they returned, but that's just not the gig?

And what happens to the relationships you make while teaching abroad?

It varies, obviously. It's not uncommon for teachers to find a future spouse (or at least partners) along the way, but that's nothing out of the ordinary for a job. What makes teaching unique is the glimpse it gives you into a person's life before circumstances speed them away from you; it's like looking into the windows of a train as it crawls past a station at night: a gallery of portraits whose characters you only see once before they're carried off into the dark.

There's a stereotype that Japanese people love taking pictures and I can testify first-hand that it's true. Even students who only came for two or three classes with me wouldn't leave without a proper goodbye ceremony: a smattering of gifts ostentatiously wrapped and the inevitable pictures together. I must've shown up in over 100 different photos for the year I was in Japan, but somehow it was the student I liked the most whose picture I never got.

She was my last student of the week—a middle school girl whose parents had pushed her from an early, early age to learn English. As a result, she spoke impeccably well. She was almost intimidating for how intelligent she was. Conversation for her consisted of topics taken from the newspaper, the different challenges her teachers had specially assigned her, and a lot about art.

She laughed at my jokes, and that alone was *huge* for me because *no one else* laughed at my jokes—not the secretary, not my co-workers, not my students, no one. No one else would invent stories with me either. No one else would spend a class drawing a sea turtle resort on the board with me. Since she was the last student of the day, I could let our class go over the allotted time. Rather than the usual 1 hour, we often spent two or even three together just talking.

I adored her. And, looking back, I realize a lot of that was due to me being starved for company. I had sparse Skype calls with family or friends back home. My outings with students were never fully satisfying because of how different we were. Out of all that, I had at least one person to connect with.

We exchanged drawings off and on. Most were just doodles of animals, but in the last class we traded pictures that must've taken us hours apiece to make. I gave her a massive collage that incorporated all the memorable elements of my experience in Japan: a blow fish, the lantern festival, mountains, and at the center—tying it all together with a Celtic knot—a horse. She gave me a horse too, only hers was connected to a globe around which there was a patterning of animals and objects we had discussed in our time together. I carry that with me wherever I go —it was on my wall in Mexico, Colorado, and it went with me to Russia too.

She left without a way to find her—no Facebook, no cell number, no email—and even if she had, it would be weird to reinitiate contact. What would I say? "Remember me? The interloper who only spent a handful of hours during a year with you? The dude who developed a weird fondness for your company for lack of any other human contact?"

Nah. Like ours, a lot of these relationships are just contextual. Take yourself out of that foreign environment and they lose all their meaning. In a way it's better to leave them in the past— lustrously trapped in amber.

Don't trust turtles

Y'know what's a good time killer?—folktales. If you ever find yourself 15 minutes short of ending a class or just starved for good conversation, try digging a few out of your students. You can start out by mentioning the most implausible ones you know from your own background. Lumberjack tales are a great go-to for this; the Hide Behind, the Cactus Cat, whatever the heck the Gumberoo is—pull up pictures of these cryptids and you're bound to start an interesting conversation. One look at them and your students will suddenly remember "Oh, yeah. We've got this one story about a possessed umbrella that eats people..."

True story that one. Not the umbrella, obviously, but it's an actual Japanese folktale. There's also one about a rock which was also a ghost—a rock-ghost—that I never fully understood. My student tried her best to explain it through drawings and limited English, but all I ended up with was a rock with a face on it that looked like a lopsided smiley face. Understanding wasn't necessarily the final goal, though, it was really more of a cultural exchange (psst, see how I passed off a botched communication as "culture" there for lack of anything else to call it?), and ultimately I was just building rapport and killing time anyway.

Above all, it was fun. And that's what we hope for from most of our stories, isn't it? They're something we can enjoy listening to and something we can enjoy retelling—a real twofer. In the spirit of that, I wanna share with you the story of Urashima Taro. For brevity's sake, we'll call him Turtle Boy since you probably won't remember his real name anyway.

Turtle Boy was a fisherman from a little coastal village in ancient Japan. True to the time period and its lack of child labor laws, he was a breadwinner for his family. Every day he'd go out fishing in his little boat and bring back whatever he caught for dinner. One day he was walking along the shore when he came across a group of kids sadistically torturing a turtle. Not being a sadist himself, he rescued this turtle and set about returning it to the ocean.

And wouldn't you know it? It was a magic turtle. It started talking to him and was all like "You saved me, kind sir! In recognition of your selflessness, I want to invite you to the kingdom of the Turtle Princess!" At this point either the turtle exploded to ten times its size or Turtle Boy shrank down to a tenth of his own. Either way, the next thing he knew he was riding on its back to the Turtle Kingdom.

Once he got to the Turtle Kingdom, Turtle Boy was introduced to the Turtle Princess who praised him: "You're a pretty cool guy. You should stay and check out the Turtle Kingdom, we'll even cover your room and board." Turtle Boy was understandably concerned about getting back to his wretchedly poor family, but who would turn down an all expenses paid vacation, much less to a mystical kingdom under the sea? As anyone would, he accepted.

This conversation played out the same way over the next few days. Turtle Boy would marvel at the wonders of the Kingdom, return to the Princess, and decide to stay another day. This could only go on for so long, though; his guilt eventually got the better of him and he finally decided it was time to go home. At this point the Princess bade him farewell and gave him a parting gift: "Here's a lovely ornamental box. NEVER OPEN IT."

Nowadays we've all been spoiled into believing skepticism is healthy, but Turtle Boy accepted this without question. With the box under his arm, he mounted a turtle and returned to land. The sight which he came upon, though, was drastically different from what he remembered: the trees were taller, sparser, or just seemed to be in the wrong place; there were houses and roads where he'd never seen them before. He wandered down the coast to where his family lived, but everything seemed foreign to him—even the people. They looked at him strangely for his outfit and he at them for theirs. Their speech was outlandish if intelligible at all.

Working up his courage, he eventually spoke to one of these strangers and asked what anyone would've asked in his situation "Where am I?" The man responded with a place name that he had never heard before, so Turtle Boy's rejoinder, naturally, was "You mean this isn't X village?" "No. Definitely not," replied the man. "That's a name which hasn't been used for at least 100 years."

And then it hit him: 100 years. He'd stayed in the Turtle Kingdom for 10 days. With each day that had passed beneath the waves, on land it must've been…

And almost unconsciously, he reached for the box the Turtle Princess had given him. Even though she'd told him never to open it, he was desperate. "Surely there must be some answer here," he thought. He pried open the lid, air rushed in as if a vacuum seal had been broken, and then—*muku muku muku muku*—purplish smoke rose slowly out of the box towards him. It enveloped him, sank into him, and as it did he felt himself aging. When the wind finally blew it away, he found himself 100 years older and stranded as a stranger in his own land.

The moral?

Turtles are jerks. Don't do anything for them. Don't trust them. Don't accept gifts from them. Just don't mess with them. Just don't. Period. If there's a hero in this story, then it's probably the boys who were torturing the turtle in the beginning. Served him right.

Nah, I have no idea. Like a lot of Japanese folk stories I've heard, the moral always seems to be "The world will do with you what it will," which sounds about right. Far from these abstract musings, though, what was going through my mind as I listened wasn't "Wow, what a delightful, yet sadly fatalistic story," but rather "I hope the knife which is slowly twisting itself into my stomach will stop soon because it's hard to keep this smile plastered on my face while I feel like I'm being stabbed from the inside out."

Well, maybe "stab" isn't the right word. It was actually more of a churning sensation. It was like putting a blender on the lowest setting possible and then feeding your intestines into the whirring blades little by little. That wasn't even the worst part about it, though. The worst part about it was that the horrible feeling I was experiencing was entirely my own fault.

When I went to Japan, I didn't know how to eat.

Granted: I understood that nutrients were obtained by placing edible objects into my mouth, masticating them, and then swallowing them rather than, say, sticking porterhouse steaks into my ear or absorbing energy from the sun like a plant. What I was never very good at, though, was figuring out how to obtain those nutrients *effectively*.

My diet in Japan largely consisted of brown rice, hard boiled eggs and coffee. If that sounds awful, it's because it was. And I was mostly aware of how awful it was thanks to instances like the aforementioned intestine smoothie.

I made various laughable attempts to combat this. I bought granola bars from the local 7-11 which, while not terrible, were hardly the same as a full course meal. I included a myriad of vegetables in my shopping trips which just sat in my fridge untouched for me to stare at in exhaustion until they got too moldy to keep. Other times I bought boxes of instant noodles which I ate between classes; these were tasty and provided a momentary jolt of energy but did nothing long-term.

And long-term energy was precisely what I needed. Firstly, I needed it to maintain my mental energy as I hopelessly continued the charade of being the cheerful, wide-eyed foreigner in an exotic land for my students' amusement; I was convinced that the students would complain and my boss would give me the boot as soon as I showed any displeasure. Secondly, I needed long-term energy to *prepare* decent food so that I would, in turn, *have* long-term energy. It was a catch-22.

There was a bigger problem at play too. Before I left for Japan, I was regularly told things to the effect of "You'll probably learn so much and it'll be such an eye-opening great experience to get away from everything you know and immerse yourself in the land of temples and mountaintops where people have tea with dragons while playing shogi unlike we do in the west where we're all so obsessed with material possessions so I hope you'll take advantage of every experience as it presents itself and learn a lot and grow as a person I wish I could do what you're doing."

I totally bought that pitch. So much so that anything *except* "total cultural immersion" felt like a failure. There were weekends where I'd have nothing to do (because, honestly, doesn't everyone have lazy weekends?) and I'd be kicking myself for not taking advantage of this "once in a lifetime ohmygod so great experience."

That same philosophy carried over to my eating too. I'd go to the supermarket and stand bewildered in an aisle consisting of *nothing* but dried mushrooms—all of which looked exactly the same—and rather than telling myself "You don't know how to eat this," I'd say "I *have* to eat this." I regularly bought, cooked, and ate bizarre things from the store just as a way of proving I wasn't being too squeamish. The results were not excellent.

At best, I'd scrape together an acceptable if somewhat disgusting dish. I once bought an octopus tentacle and boiled it for hours and hours in hopes of reducing its rubberiness until I eventually gave up and just gnawed my way through it. Another time I bought a Styrofoam tray of lantern squids and cooked them crockpot style only to discover that their eyes bulged out like little tumors as they were heated. No matter, I thought, each little pop as I chewed on them was another point for how culturally immersed I was.

I presented photographic evidence of these horrible experiments to my students for conversation. At no point, I think, did they realize how miserable I was making myself (or if they did, they certainly didn't come out and say it). Instead, they seemed impressed at how bold and creative I was. Some even egged me on. The same woman who told me the Turtle Boy story gave me a recipe for wakame salad which had me retching on the floor for an hour because apparently the dehydrated seaweed hadn't fully expanded when I ingested it. I didn't want to unduly burden her, though, so I told her "Yeah. Wow. It was delicious."

Not all my dishes were wretched failures, though. At the turn of the year, I got ideas from different students about how to make ozoni—a typical new year's soup—and that turned out pretty great, especially with a dash of hot sauce (which my students were astounded by). Another time I even made my own sushi which, while really messy and unwieldy, was still delicious.

For all my meager successes, though, I had no staple food. And *that* is the whole point here. Experimenting isn't bad. Going out of your gastronomic comfort zone isn't bad. If you don't wanna do that then you have no business going abroad in the first place. At the same time, though, there ought to be no judgment for sticking with what you know, sticking with what works. You have to think about yourself.

Another thing I did to be more "immersed" during my stay in Japan was sleeping on a futon. My apartment came with a long green one which I could fold up neatly in the closet during the daytime (just like a real Japanese person!) and I figured "Well, when in Rome..."

Anyone who uses that phrase ought to put themselves in the shoes of a Roman gladiator who just got beheaded. Or, better yet, think of the many slaves that made the Roman Empire possible. Surely that's something to aspire to in the name of cultural immersion.

As you can probably guess, the futon was not comfortable for me. Having about three or four heads of extra height on the average Japanese person, it seems ridiculous to think that I would've *ever* been comfortable sleeping on a five-inch pad. It gave me horrible back pains and I could barely sleep.

I put up with this until one day, about nine months into my stay, I woke up sick of everything and stormed off to the nearest furniture store. Short of being able to buy a full bed, I bought a second futon with the intention of stacking them. I was lugging this massive thing back through the streets of my city when I ran into the mother of one of my students. She looked at my massive futon. She looked back at me.

"NO. I *CANNOT* AND I *WILL NOT* EXIST WITH JUST ONE FUTON. REGARDLESS OF WHAT MAY BE SUFFICIENT FOR YOUR PEOPLE. STOP JUDGING ME."

That's what I mentally was saying, but of course she was just concerned about me transporting a mattress back to my house. "You live close?" she asked, to which I responded "Yes" and then I went on my merry way. That night I slept better than I had for almost a year, and all because I'd decided to ignore what others might think and stack two futons on top of each other.

Funnily enough, simple solutions like these are often the most effective. Who would've guessed it? If you go into a foreign environment like this expecting to totally reinvent yourself, though, it's no wonder that you might overcomplicate your life and subsequently suffer from stress. If you expect to have miso soup every morning instead of just standard cereal and milk but you suck at cooking, you might not have a great start to your day. If you think that you've gotta spend an hour preparing yourself a bento box instead of just slapping a sandwich together in a few minutes, you might neglect your cooking duties because you're too tired and end up trapped in a vicious cycle of *never* having enough energy.

Going back to Turtle Boy (and you thought that was just a hook, eh?), maybe the lesson you can draw from his story is one of forgetting your origins. Even though his family was at the back of his mind the whole time, he was so taken in by the exotic splendor of the Turtle Kingdom that he forgot his place in the world.

When he finally realized what was important in his life, it was too late.

When you go abroad for the first time, you can get wrapped up in this enchanting line of "I'm gonna find myself; like, who I *really* am," never realizing that you *already know* who you are. Transplanting yourself to a foreign land doesn't magically make up for your shortcomings. That line of thought is perilous because the further you follow it, the more you fill up a little box with stress & disappointment until the fateful day when it opens up and takes a hellish physical toll on you.

Before you picture the wise, cultured globe-trotter you'll be coming out on the other side of your experience, ask yourself "who am I now?" because that's who you're gonna suffer being all throughout the journey.

Just for starters: can I cook? You should at least be able to prepare an easy, nutritious meal over the weekend to be consumed for the following week. What do I need to be comfortable? How much human interaction can I tolerate before I want to rip my face off? That's something I seriously overestimated during my time in Japan. Do I know how to dress properly and do I have a decent wardrobe? I wore thrift-store clothing, cut my own hair, and never knew how to tie a tie effectively until my third year in. What's my hobby or—if my hobbies suck—how can I lie effectively about having one?

And maybe these are questions you'll answer along the way. That wouldn't be terrible. Just, above all, don't discount your own needs. We humans have a remarkable ability for making ourselves suffer needlessly. Reflect on whether or not you're doing that to yourself.

Oh, and don't trust turtles.

You are an exotic parrot

I've never been an animal salesman and I hope I never will be because the mere idea of it makes me uncomfortable. Transporting living things for the pleasure of monied individuals should make anyone with a shred of sympathy uneasy. Imagine you take a colorful bird from the tropics and bring it to the cold north where it'll live out the rest of its life in a heated apartment while snow and harsh winds pepper the landscape outside. How could you ensure that the journey from here to there wouldn't go horribly wrong? How could you capture that bird without scaring it to death? Should you? How could you ensure that it was kept within a temperature-controlled environment for the whole trip? How could you feed it and keep it from plucking off all its feathers in the ensuing stress? Obviously, the answer to all of these things is "you don't do it in the first place."

But imagine that parrot *volunteered* to go to a harsh, new climate. How would it ever cope? How would it get a passport? Clearly parrots don't have passports (as far as I know). How would it interact with the local birds? How would it learn to live off the local flora? How would it use money? Could it learn to drive a car if it could already drive a car in its home country? At this point the metaphor's kinda falling apart, but you get my point. You—as the foreign transplant teacher—are like an exotic parrot and that's how you'll be treated.

Setting aside the logistics of parrots driving cars, let's focus on the interaction side of things. When someone goes to a zoo, it's with the objective of seeing a strange, foreign animal. Likewise, you'll often be a zoo animal for your students. You'll be someone to take bragging-rights photos with. Students in your class will come to gawk and stare and there'll be no shortage of people who say "wow. Is that how they do things in your country?!" for something as banal as the way you open a window.

What's more, you know how people are always trying to teach parrots new words? That'll be your experience with the local language. Sometimes students will repeat words at you as if they're speaking to a toddler and, should you ever reproduce a word, you'll be able to say the most unremarkable things to a round of gasps and applause. This applies even if you've got a working proficiency in the language. I recall a time I was in front of a class of teacher trainees in Mexico who asked me to say something in Spanish. I had a C1 level at that point and could've said any number of impressive phrases, but the only thing that came to mind was "my elbow hurts." The resulting astonishment from the class would've made you think that I'd just pronounced a testament on the rights of man.

On special occasions you may also get wheeled out for entertainment purposes. The school I worked for in Japan, for example, had numerous parties and outings that I was expected to participate in. There were two separate parties for Christmas and Halloween (one for adults and another for children) and we were never short on students who wanted to rent me out for a weekend to go to a cave or a mountain.

You'll also get more handsy types who want to grab at you just like a child would grab at a brightly colored object. One girl I taught had an obsession with my arm hair and used to abruptly stroke it while whispering "wow. It's like a cat."

Conversely, just as there are those who get bored with zoos because the elephant is always an elephant and the giraffe is always a giraffe, you'll have students who get bored with you. Globalization has made great strides in disillusioning us all: I don't even care for zoos anymore because I can already find a range of exotic animals doing entertaining things through a mere YouTube search (and for free, to boot). The North American and British semi-aquatic hairless ape are particularly well documented in this way: their songs are broadcasted across the airwaves of practically every country on earth, their faces and habits the subject of nearly every type of popular media.

And you—being a typical member of this group—won't even represent the best of us. Don't be surprised if the "culture" you've come to dispense is regarded as old hat, especially by the newer generations. Teenagers will think of you as little more than an annoying blaring sound in the background of a place they're forced to go to twice a week by their parents. After all the attention of the looky-loos, though, it's a relief.

Even so, don't discount the value of your exotic appeal. When I applied for the JET Program, part of the interview was role-playing the first day of work. The interviewers pretended to be Japanese students and I was supposed to introduce myself. I just said predictable stuff like "hi, I'm Iain. I'm from Colorado. We're famous for mountains and skiing. I'm pleased to meet you all" and so on.

Not terrible. But not excellent either.

Back in the days of kings and queens, what did envoys of foreign kingdoms always bring each other?—gifts. Gifts transcend language barriers. Gifts made a good first impression, not only of the giver but also of where the giver came from.

Now I'm not saying that you *have* to buy *everyone* exotic souvenirs, but it does pay off to do it with a few people. I started off my job in Japan by giving my coworkers tea and buffalo bars from Colorado—they were cheap, non-perishable, and they immediately said "I come from a land of plenty. I am a worker of plenty."

Beyond that, you're obviously not gonna buy buffalo bars for the fifty-some students you'll have. In that case, *you* are the gift. Think about it: at some point, we've all lingered absent-mindedly on the different countries on a map and wondered "what goes on there, anyway?" We can look up a Wikipedia article on it, watch a YouTube video (which, I'm not ashamed to say, I do regularly), but the Internet hasn't (yet) displaced the value of actually *meeting* a living person from that far-off land.

Play that up. If I had to do my JET Program interview over again, y'know what I'd do? I'd load up on those quarters—the ones that have a picture dedicated to every state on the back of them—

and I'd just pass them around with no more of an introduction than "this is where I'm from."

It's an exaggeration, granted, but measured realism is what Wikipedia articles are for. You're better than that. People will love you for the same reason people love parrots: because they're colorful, vibrant, expressive, exotic. People will be bored by you for the same reason they're bored by parrots: because they're *nothing but* colorful, vibrant, expressive, exotic.

"PROFESSIONAL" ADVICE

Why there are no "good teachers"

Let's rattle off some classroom variables: how much time did you put into the lesson? Did the students do the homework? Did everyone bring their book? Is everyone in a good mood or is someone hungry? Is someone huffy because someone else stole their usual seat? Does your textbook CD actually work or is the single track you need scratched? Have the students already learned the material at their normal school? Is the textbook interesting or outdated and poorly sequenced? Is there an odd number of students? Are the desks arranged so that everyone can see the board? Is there enough light in the classroom? Is there a weird smell? Are all the chairs the same color? Did someone track mud onto the floor? Do you have enough markers? Did you make enough copies? Is one of the students going to go ballistic because he didn't get the answers as quickly as the others and start strangling his neighbor?

Everything mentioned here represent legitimate problems I've had. Even the slightest change in the delicate ecosystem of a classroom can spell disaster for a class. I once observed a woman teaching a class focused on pronunciation that would've been solid minus the fact that the lights were dim; all the students were falling asleep and she, panicking because she thought they were bored, sped through it all before they could process the material. More than once in Japan, my students responded to the question "how was your weekend?" with "my aunt/uncle/brother/mother/father/goldfish died." "Oh," I responded, "I'm so sorry" (though secretly I was cursing my luck, knowing full well the nosedive the class was about to take). Another time my biweekly teens, jaded from an onslaught of finals, decided their time was better spent playing their water bottles like a Peruvian flute band than learning the "I wish" structure. I wish they hadn't had finals that particular week, but how was I to know?

Oftentimes you simply don't. Preparing a top-notch class is kind of like preparing a top-notch suit: for as snazzy as it looks, there's no guaranteeing the people in it will be snazzy too.

This is why I balk at the term "good teacher." There are good planners, good emergency response experts, but since teaching is a two-way street, there's nothing that ensures a class will go well, students will learn, or someone won't burst into tears at a perceived slight.

Remember how I mentioned the color of chairs in the classroom? If you've got a class with really little kids, chances are they'll fight over who gets to sit in the blue chair and who gets the pink one. Ditto with markers—even magnets provoke temper tantrums.

Remember how I mentioned the number of students? If you've got an odd number, then pair activities (which make up pretty much *every* conversation activity in a textbook) will be super awkward. Either you'll swapping partners around like an octopus puppet show or you (*the teacher*) will wind up talking to someone in place of another student (take too long, though, and the others will finish before you, generating a period of dead air where people start goofing off or just get moody and vindictive).

Remember how I mentioned the number of copies? If you're just starting a course, chances are the students won't all have the book—i.e. you'll be making copies. You'll start out teaching a few students according to your plan, but then your coordinator will pop her head in to say "Surprise! You've actually got eight students, not five!" You'll ask the one student with a book to share with the newcomers, or maybe ask them to share copies, only to discover that they're unwilling to do so. Some people can be weirdly territorial with their books; the second you look away, they'll yank it away from their partner or force them to go through some Cirque du Soleil level contortions across the desk just to read the text.

I could go on (AND I'D LIKE TO because complaining about work has become a pitiful hobby of mine), but you get the point: everything you do as a teacher is a gamble. Hence, I discourage you from ever aspiring to be a "good" teacher. Be an adaptable teacher. Recognize the elements of chaos at work in the classroom. Anticipate them. Prepare for them. Above all:

don't be surprised if everything blows up in your face.

It's a steady slope to madness

You know that monk that lit himself on fire to protest the war in Vietnam? That guy from Rage Against the Machine's first album? That guy would've been a "good teacher."

Why? Because teaching is akin to self-immolation. If you're a dedicated teacher (and of course you are, why would they hire you if you weren't?) then you'll constantly be looking for ways to improve your classes. Coordinators, bosses, observers, workshop hosts, TED Talk speakers, and all the like will push you down that road, but let me tell you: it has no end.

There are days when I question if I'm missing that extra special something. Do we need more work with reading and, if so, should I find some articles to adapt? Do the kids want more games or should I bury them in worksheets to get the grammar across? Should I be more strict with my teens? Does that upper intermediate class deserve a podcast assignment to keep them enthusiastic? Should I establish ironclad rules and bring them to class on poster boards like Moses descending Mount Sinai to smash the golden ass with his tablets?

Oftentimes these questions are a bitter reflection following a particularly bad class. They're useful—and they motivate me to change things for the better—but the thing is that they never stop. It's a steady slope to madness if you continually follow the "what could I do better?" line of thought.

At my first job they gave me a key to the school with the understanding that I could go in and out whenever I wanted. This I did regularly. I was the first to arrive and the last to leave almost every day; I was even there on weekends when no one else was. I was more than happy to take advantage of the office's unlimited Wi-Fi (they only sprang for 8 GB a month in my apartment), but the real reason for my "diligence" was much simpler—guilt.

Nothing I did seemed to work. Whatever copies I'd made, whatever meticulous lesson plan I'd crafted, whatever original materials I'd prepared always ended up discarded in a folder. The rare times we DID use what I'd made, I got nothing but apathy or confusion in response.

I once went so far as to write and produce an original dialogue. I wrote the script and accompanying activities in November. My dad recorded the audio with a friend who even included ambient sound effects. I edited the resulting mp3. I drew pictures on the board three different times to set the context (including a house with painstakingly rendered shingles) and three different times had to erase it all because the class got off track or the students arrived late. It wasn't until after Christmas break that I finally debuted my masterpiece only to be flatly told "No. We can't understand it because the bird song in the background is too loud." In a last-ditch effort, I performed the whole thing myself using my hands as sock puppets. I got some laughs, but that was about it. No one was in awe of my in situ examples of how to use the word "get" for 10 different functions, nor did they inquire about where it had come from. Everything was just business as usual.

As I would only realize later, the deck was stacked against me. My school professed to take a learning through conversation approach, but how this actually worked was anyone's guess. No one bothered to consider that an elementary student who can't even say what she had for lunch won't be able to shoot the breeze with a native speaker. For this, and of course for kids, we were sheepishly offered textbooks, but it was always emphasized that half of the class should be free conversation. From there, we had 30 minutes to cover new material--at best.

One hour a week with no study plan, no homework, and little to no new language input was a fool's errand from the start. No one can learn effectively with that, but I was too dumb to realize it at the time.

I clung to the belief that all those rainy Sunday nights in the office would amount to something. I whittled down my weekends to just one day so that the other could be spent poring over our meager textbooks in search of something—anything—that might inspire enthusiasm. All the while, the last trains of the evening rattled around the bend of the mountain range; the lights of the station across the road went dark; storefront shutters dropped; and the lights of the lonely stoplight filled the room as I labored into night. Things were as they were.

The sad thing about all this was that I was actually working against myself. The reason so little got done in my job was because nothing was meant to be done. The school was selling an experience, not knowledge. Many of our clients were housewives who, in my boss's words, had fantasies about hanging out with a handsome foreigner. They just wanted to spend time with their friends pursuing a casual hobby and there I was with my textbook copies and mini-grammar lessons impeding any chance of that. The ideal employee would've been a bubbly fountain of charm and anecdotes, not a teacher. Had I had spent my weekends touring nearby cities and bringing back pictures and souvenirs to share, everyone would've been much happier—most importantly myself.

No TEFL preparation course worth its price tag will tell you just to be a chummy tourist, though—not in a million years—and for good reason. Your most valued service ought to be teaching. That was the confounding thing for me. Even so, what I learned from my first job is that you, as a tourist, are sometimes just as valuable as a teacher.

The siren song of "what could I do better?" is a constant lure for a teacher who actually values their job. Administration will even encourage it with trainings, offerings of extra materials, and suggestions for extra class hours. Like Odysseus, you can choose to hear it all out; but, also like Odysseus, you ought to plug your men's ears with bee's wax and tie yourself to the mast first.

Teaching is a consuming job. It consumes not just *time* but *you* as well. In Mexico, I gave classes to teachers from the local university once a week. They struck me as busy at first, but the extent of their job never hit home until one of them had a nervous breakdown. Naturally, he quit the course, but it was strange for me to think that he—a person who always seemed cheerful and cooperative—could've gone overboard. As my colleague later explained, though, teachers like him often fielded up to 40 hours of class a week. Stretch that among the obligatory half of contact hours necessary for good planning (20 hours), with a family, administrative tasks, commuting, and everything in between and you've got a recipe for disaster.

My dad is another good example of this. When people ask me what the biggest contributor to global warming is, I say him. I swear he's put more smoke into the atmosphere than all the factories of the Industrial Revolution combined. Beer bottles too —he's contributed a staggering amount of those to the planet. Taking out his garbage on Tuesday nights was always like clearing the floor of a cheap sailors' bar with a push broom. He must've smoked a pack a day and had at least 2 or 3 beers a night.

Looking back, though, I recognize he almost needed those addictions. He worked at one of the lowest performing high schools in Colorado, woke up at 6 every morning to drive into Denver, stayed up past midnight each night grading papers, and played host to principals who hadn't taught a day in their life, immigrant children who didn't speak English, and the occasional oddball who was expelled for bringing a sword to school. To stay in a job like that you need to care, and that was precisely my dad's problem: he cared.

Many people treat teaching like any other job: they assume that 40 hours of class a week is perfectly fine because, after all, that's the same as a standard 9 to 5 weekday job. The downside of teaching, though, is that you take it home with you. You don't just have to grade and plan; you also load up emotional baggage. Every cross student, every disruptive smart aleck, every class clown, every troubled child, every incompetent boss— you hold them up like Atlas holds the world. For that reason alone, you're entitled to a break.

A friend of mine put it best when she said that your life is a patchwork of squares. You've got your social squares for friends, lovers and family; then there are your private squares, your work square, your hobby squares, etc. These squares can grow and shrink according to how much attention you give them. We should all strive to have some balance among them, but the problem with the teaching square is that it consumes all the others—if you let it.

Let your teaching square grow a little if necessary. Do that little bit extra if it pleases you. Be the super teacher (yay, you). But *don't,* don't let yourself be consumed. A teacher who cares should just as well be a teacher who cares for himself.

Everyone can learn English, even those who can't

Camus says that we have to imagine Sisyphus as happy—just cheerfully chugging his boulder up that hellish incline day-after-day until the end of time, never once discouraged by it rolling all the way back to the bottom. Supposedly that's the trick to absurdism. You free yourself from the depressing entanglements of reality by letting yourself *get* entangled and being happy about it.

And why not? You see that boulder go tumbling back down the hill enough times and it's bound to be funny eventually.

Fill in this blank: "my father ___ a doctor." Did you answer "is?" Good for you! I bet you recognized that you were using the third person present conjugation of the to be verb after thoroughly analyzing the sentence and realizing that, in the absence of another verb, it was unnecessary to use "do" and that, due to the absence of a direct object such as "breakfast" or "bike," it was additionally unnecessary to include or conjugate the verb "eat" or "ride" into "eats" or "rides." Moreover, kudos on not seeing the word "my," thinking "I," and subsequently saying "my father am a doctor."

You probably didn't understand any of that technobabble. If you did, it's because you're unfortunate enough to have sunk incomprehensibly into the jargony depths of teaching; elsewise, you wouldn't need it. Even teaching-wise, it's arguable whether that wheelbarrow of semantic junk is necessary. What something *is* or *isn't* is a basic concept that we should all understand as humans.

You'd think. Give this to a group of children, though, and they'll give you wonders such as "my father are a doctor" or "my father what a doctor" or maybe even "my father his a doctor." It gets hysterical sometimes, especially after you've done this same exercise for six or seven different classes.

But how on earth did you get here? Well, you started out by drilling the "he/she/it = is" mantra after the book introduced professions and family members. "My aunt is a chef, my brother is a pilot." You contrasted this with "I am a student, I am a teacher." You wrote this in beautifully color-coordinated columns on the board. They did the listening. They connected the family members with the corresponding professions. Everything seemed hunky-dory. But then, when the cloze activity came out, suddenly the "aunt am a doctor" and the "dad dad a banker."

You reviewed it the next class. The same thing happened: "the brother are a pilot, she am I." The snarky Russian grammar teacher lectures you on how Russian doesn't use the to be verb, so of course they don't understand it—something you already knew from studying your basic Russian textbook. The students go to her for a first language grammar lesson. They come back with the grammar teacher's smug assurance that she sorted it all out, yet more "I are a teacher. You am a student" follows.

"No!" you shout. "*I* am a teacher. *You* are a student." "*I* am a teacher. *You* are a student," the students eerily parrot back. "No! *You! You!*" "Youyouyou," they mechanically rattle back at you.

Fast forward a couple of weeks and it's the same story. You're laboriously putting together a PowerPoint with arrows, speech bubbles, and pictures which will make the associations clear, you hope, but this is your umpteenth attempt. There have been numerous worksheets, games, individual tutorings, homework assignments, even you translating the sentence directly from their mother tongue, thrusting out Google Translate on your phone like Frodo warding off Shelob with the phial of Galadriel. Nothing works.

You contact your academic supervisor and wrangle an observation out of him, hoping he'll point you in the right direction, also terrified that the students will suddenly "get it" and you'll just look crazy. But, no. The same are-ing and am-ing plays out and he, for his part, just shrugs. "Maybe these kids will be great hair stylists or scientists, but language just isn't their thing.

Stick it out"

You're not allowed to say it, but some students just won't learn. I wouldn't go so far as to say *can't* learn, because it's largely a question of effort, but there are always gonna be deadweights. You get your boulder. You push it up the hill. You laugh it off every time it plunges back down.

Children have a mental block. They haven't learned to think analytically, so it's a shot in the dark as to whether they get the language or not. You can dress it up with puppets, kinesthetic activities, songs, colors, pictures, whatever, but it's hard to tell what the magic bullet will be (or if there is one). As for teenagers, they've got a mental block called being a teenager.

Lemme tell you about "corner girl." She and I worked together from the beginning to the end of my time in Mexico (two years over the course of different classes). What was unerring about her? Her ability to do nothing. She arrived thirty minutes to an hour late for every class I had, sat in the corner, and wouldn't participate unless directly asked to. Whenever she arrived it was like a lazy rain cloud floated into the otherwise cheerful ambience of the room.

If she spent her time idly chatting like a normal teenager, I wouldn't've been surprised, but she didn't even do that. She just lounged there like a stagnant puddle some sick cosmic joke had granted sentience. In every course, she either failed or just barely scraped by.

At first, I suspected she had a disorder of some kind, but no one could confirm or deny that and, at any rate, she seemed mostly normal. If she had been younger (around 14ish) I could've dismissed it as teenage apathy, but this chick was an *undergraduate*. Moreover, she came of her own volition. Who does that? From occasional conversations I learned she was studying architecture but I could not—for the life of me—perceive any way in which English benefited her.

But, hey. She paid good money to come sit in a corner for four hours every weekend. Far be it from me to say she couldn't squander her resources however she pleased. That, at least, was how it worked from the school's perspective and I, as an employee there, had no choice but to agree. I gave my classes, watched everything bounce off her apathetic shell, tried in vain to draw her into activities, cheered her on, and then I slapped an F on her final. Circle of life.

Funnily enough, you'll even get adults who won't learn sometimes and not always for lack of trying. The oldest student I've ever taught was 86 years old. She relied heavily on hearing aids (two until a thief stole one of them) which whined shrilly throughout the class. Any conversation with her was pretty much "how was your weekend?" "EH!?" "HOW WAS YOUR WEEKEND?" "EH!?" "HOW WAS YOUR—" "WEEKEND!?" "YES!"

English was a hobby for her. Prior to the war, as she told me, there was no English anywhere, but now that it was everywhere, she'd decided to learn it. Inspiring, no? As a story, it's great. I gloss over it whenever anyone asks me to share my hallmark moments in teaching. What I don't go into is the details of what the classes were like.

There wasn't really any goal with her. There was no textbook, no test, job or vacation she was studying for; i.e. progress was pretty much nil. Every Thursday she'd bring me a baked yam or some other vegetable from her garden, and we'd shout our way through a conversation that neither of us had the vocabulary for.

It got to be pretty nice, actually. No one in my training course ever told me how to trade conversation for yams, but I got the hang of it. The key was just accepting that we weren't going anywhere. Another week, another time up the hill.

Interrogation techniques

Y'know that cliché scene out of police dramas where the cops have the bad guy in the interrogation room—the classic metal table, metal chairs, two-way mirror? Y'know how the hard-boiled detective storms into the room and he's all like "WHERE ARE THEY?!" as he proceeds to hurl a chair across the room? Y'know how he'll proceed to smash the villain's head against the table, pull his hair, yell death threats and all the other typical shenanigans?

That's what most speaking activities are like in the classroom. Only with a couple key differences: first, you don't get to throw things and smash heads (but, oh, how you'll want to); second, you don't get to yell or make death threats (but, oh, how you'll want to). Instead, you'll just have to sit there smiling, asking innocuous questions like "How was your weekend? What's your favorite flavor of ice cream? Have you gone to the cinema recently?" and so on. I'm hoping someday there'll be an interrogation scene where the militant cop screams all that—furniture chucking and all—but it's probably never gonna happen.

So, speaking—it can be a royal pain. The other skills are far more manageable. Listening activities create a magical hush in the classroom while everyone strains to understand British people talking about their daily lives (who'd've guessed it?). Reading is just something you do at home; if the students don't do it, then it's their problem. Writing is the tagalong friend that everyone forgets about and conveniently abandons at the first opportunity; you can justify letting it slide with a "C'mon, guys; this isn't Shakespeare."

No such luck with speaking. Speaking is precisely what rich, ambitious parents will be sending their kids to learn. Speaking is the ultimate validation of language ability. When we want to know if someone can handle a foreign language, we don't ask "Can you *write* English? Can you *read* English?" No, no. We say "Can you *speak* it?"

In short: speaking is important. It's also the hardest thing to implement in a classroom. Unlike doing a worksheet or a listening activity, speaking requires effort. It's a series of mental gymnastics your students'll do painfully slowly, all the while conscious of their classmates sniggering at mispronunciations.

If you win the cosmic lottery, you might get a classroom full of mixed language students. It's a beautiful thing, that. If everyone's hobbled by having different languages, the only possible way to communicate becomes English—and *that* is a powerful motivator. More often, though, you'll wind up with monocrop students who'll blow off talking to each other in English because "pfft. We already can communicate effectively in our own language."

That leaves the onus on you to motivate (or, more likely *force*) the use of English in the classroom. Everyone has their own ways to do this but, for what it's worth, here I'd like to share some of my own. As I see it, the key problems with speaking activities are, as illustrated above, the strain involved and the potential for embarrassment; any good speaking activity should therefore strive to minimize these. Take, for example:

- **Revolving pairs:** if you've got a list of questions in the textbook which say "discuss with your partner" (and you will), don't waste your time. In most cases the students will blow through everything in a minute or two with grunts and "I don't knows." No. Instead, stand everyone up, set a timer for about a minute, make everyone find a partner, then start the discussion; every time the timer rolls over, have everyone move to the next question with a new partner. The beauty of this method is that you can control the group's progression as a whole: no one finishes early because they're slacking off, no one feels singled out because they're *actually doing* the activities. If you've got a big group, you can even repeat the exercise with new pairs.

- **Word Carousel:** an alternative to the revolving pairs, you can use this with more detail-specific activities. Put a bunch of papers on the walls with a prompt and blank spaces; students circulate around the room in pairs, adding their own sentences to the papers. If you're teaching "can/can't" in conjunction with "places around town," for example, you can write "in the park…," "at the theater…," "at school…," etc. on a bunch of papers and stick them on the walls. As the students go round in pairs, they'll have to discuss what to write for each place while also reading what others have written—e.g. "you can read a book," "you can see a shark." After the pages are full, you can take them down, redistribute them and extend the activity with a "do you agree or disagree" session or some other thing.
- **Pictures:** wherever you get them from is fine, be it loose magazines, the students' phones (they're lying if they say they don't have an internet connection, don't be fooled), or—if you're really strapped for material—just from the textbook itself (don't be afraid to flip around, it's full of pictures). Pictures are a marvelous facilitator of discussion; they give you the perfect out when the conversation goes south—can't think of any good response? Just point to something else and say, "Hey, look at that!"
- **Randomized Q&A:** get some dice. They'll never fail you. In lieu of that, get a cube and just write junk on it. Things like spinners (either from a website or made of paper) also work. Coins can be used for positives and negatives. Assign the dice values like "what/where/when/why/who/how" or "he/she/I/you/they/we" and get the students to make

sentences. It doesn't matter if the answers are as flippant as "why are you not a sandwich?" or "how is he a doctor?" It's even better that way, in fact. It takes the edge off expecting the student to produce completely original material.

- **Sarcasm:** nowadays it's hip for textbooks to include a "Real-life English!" section in each unit, usually buried at the end, as if the writers were half-aware of how cringe-worthy they could be. I kid you not, you'll sometimes get a listening with two teens discussing "the best present to get for mom" in "aw, shucks" tones saying things like "a card would be BRILLIANT" or "wouldn't it be FAB if we got 'er a keychain?" Additional words like AWESOME and WICKED are indiscriminately heaped on top of these in a box labeled YOUTHFUL INFORMAL TERMS FOR EXPRESSING APPRECIATION OF POSITIVE QUALITIES or some other wad of technical jargon.

This isn't terrible for adults, but asking teens to see the value in them is a lost cause. If we could skip them altogether, that'd be FAB; unfortunately, though, they always show up on the unit tests. So, how do you combat the collective groan that always comes with this section? By acknowledging it with sarcasm, of course. With the "present for mom" thing, for example, it's already stupid to conduct a speaking activity with the book's provided examples of roses and chocolates; why not push that stupidity to the next level? Replace the roses with a broken bucket. Replace the chocolates with a stuffed deer head. Go to Google Images and print out a bunch of worthless odds and ends: a Sony Walkman from 1975, a three-legged dog, a tire iron, a cow wearing a wig.

Bring those into class and what was once a sucky activity becomes a fun opportunity for jokes—vocab included.

You might've noticed that all these activities presuppose a classroom full of young, recalcitrant and disrespectful students, i.e. teens or children. And right you are—with that lot you can never expect speaking to go smoothly. Some form of gimmickry is necessary.

Adults, on the other hand, require an adjustment of your own attitude. For that, read the next section.

Don't be a sad sack

Did I mention that I got where I am by stumbling and bungling?

Well, my first job interview is a great example of that. In my last year of college, I applied for the JET program—an operation set up by the Japanese government that ships English speakers to different schools around Japan (usually in the sticks) where they can work for a few years as teaching assistants. It's a great program; no small wonder that so many people apply and are turned down each year.

I was determined to get in, though. I polished my application essay to the point where just the few sentences made you go "wow." I researched all the different prefectures—even memorized their names—to get a sense of where I could be best placed. I read up on current Japanese news because rumor had it that sometimes the interviewers would ask about that. I learned some basic Japanese because, as those same rumors had it, there would be a bonus points section where I could demonstrate my ability to ask for help at gas stations or buy things at a supermarket. I had it nailed; on top of all that, I was a straight-A student and I was taking the CELTA at the same time. They'd be stupid *not* to take me.

The big day came and I swaggered off to my interview—stuffed into a suit that they must've thought I'd pinched off a dead guy. Sure enough, the interviewers were dazzled by my essay; I had written about my family's love of books and they proceeded to ask me if there were any poems I could recommend for a class. I responded that, yes, there were many good poems in my favorite book *Spoon River Anthology* which I would love to share. One in particular which sprang to mind was about a snake which climbed a tree to devour a nest of chicks, impaled their mother on a branch, and then fell itself onto the rocks below and summarily died.

There were probably several reasons I didn't get the job. I also remarked that I was a good choice for country living because

I had—get this—made many friends in my own neighborhood by helping people with building fences and storing hay in their barns. Then there was the question about current events: I dunno how I trailed off onto the topic of the American imposed no war clause in Japan's constitution, but let's just say I was screwed the second I brought it up. What *really* cinched it, though, was definitely the bird kebab.

That's not what I remember as my greatest failing, though. To this day, the question that really haunts me was much more innocuous. "What's your hobby?" Here I was all prepared with rehearsed dates about Japanese history, and carefully practiced penmanship to spell out my name in katakana and, wouldn't you know it, they ask me the one stupidly simply question I hadn't prepared for. I had hobbies, of course, but not the kind of hobbies you talk about with any degree of pride. I played video games. I watched Star Trek. I read *Spoon*-freaking-*River Anthology*.

I kicked myself for a long time after that. It was a mystery to me how all my other qualifications had lined up perfectly, yet the one thing I could never get was *fun*. That wasn't the end to my woes either. When I actually *got* a job in Japan, I guess I expected to waltz into a professional environment where everyone would ask me "Thomas sensei, would you be so kind as to explain the usages of the present subjunctive in English?" at which point I, puffing up my chest in pride, would saunter over to the whiteboard and jot out a series of startlingly enlightening example sentences which would make the audience swoon "ooooooooh!"

Instead, I was shooed into a small room where an old woman with a baked sweet potato was waiting to show me pictures of her puppies. Worst of all, my arch nemesis was lurking under the surface of every conversation: "and what's *your* hobby? What do *you* do for fun? Did *you* have a nice weekend?" (Surprise: I still had no good answer).

For a long time, I thought it was just me—which made the whole thing even worse—but that was until I read *Tonoharu*. That manga was introduced to me as being about my life—and aptly so because it could easily be retitled as *Sad Sack in Japan*.

It's about a recent college grad named Daniel who goes to work as a teaching assistant in the boonies of Japan. In his first classes he has to give a presentation about himself. He's got some pictures of his family, his sister's cat which likes to sleep in the sink, he says which state he comes from and why it's special; he rattles through all this material in a carefully rehearsed two minute presentation and then, with the rest of the class ahead of them, the teacher says "great, Dan! What's the next activity?" To which he replies "uh..."

A lot of the first book is just about him trying to fill a class with his self-introduction. He gets help from another teacher, a girl he wants to score with but does a piss-poor job of courting, and she astutely points out that there's nothing actually about *him* in the presentation. It's all about his sister's cat and his home state. "What's your hobby?" she asks him, and he responds "I guess... sleeping? watching TV?"

She knows he's not gonna win any friends with that answer, so she advises him to lie. She does it all the time, after all, because sometimes the truth just isn't interesting. At a loss for what else to do, he takes her suggestion. He proceeds to tell everyone that his hobby is *skydiving*, a lie that he has to keep up for all the following classes, inventing answers to questions about rental procedures and prices on the fly.

Whether it's in a job interview or a classroom, you've gotta sell yourself. There's an element of exaggeration and even lying that goes into that, but it all starts from an honest base where you can say "this is me. This is why you should like me." And that's, perhaps, the most important lesson I've gotten out of teaching.

I'll confess. I also applied for the Peace Corps in my last year of college, and I was rejected on the same grounds—for being a sad sack. They took one look at me and wrote me off as a wet blanket—unfit for the stress and challenge of living in an alien environment. I can't say they were totally wrong either because my sales pitch was always "I exist. Give me work and I will work."

There was a conference I went to during that application process where various vets talked about their experiences working abroad. One of them, a guy who had worked in Thailand, admitted during a speech that he couldn't claim to have achieved *anything* during his time there—he couldn't return home with the bragging rights of having built a well or established a school. His single accomplishment was simply having lived there.

But that was okay. Ultimately, he said, the people he worked with wouldn't reminisce about how he had improved the GDP of their economy by 3.26% or reduced general illiteracy across rural communities, they would reminisce about the time everyone had a race to see who could plant the most rice in a day and he had lost to the grandma. He had rolled with the punches, had simply *been* there—and that was what really mattered.

I made a commitment to breaking out of my shell while I was in Japan. I accepted every invitation I was given and tried to avoid staying at home over the weekend, even though that was still more my style. I came to almost every class with photographic evidence of me in a new place as if to proclaim "HA, HA! YOU SEE? I ALSO AM CAPABLE OF HAVING FUN! LOOK! LOOK! JUST LOOK AT MY EXPRESSION AND THE AMUSEMENT IT INDICATES!"

A lot of it was forced, obviously, but the material was a lifesaver. According to the model of the school, we were supposed to spend half the class just chatting and then, if there was time, we would do work from the textbook. The textbook was a death sentence, though, because no one had the fundaments of knowledge from previous chapters (or even before the book) to comprehend the material therein. Chatting away the hour was least painful option available for everyone.

And not just in Japan—that strategy of throwing away a class to free conversation served me well in later jobs. As anyone who has taught groups during flu season or a few days prior to vacations can testify, there are days when you wait around for 15 minutes only to have one out of a group of five come for class. Knowing you were only five minutes away from having a free period, you silently curse them for coming at all, even more so because usually they're the weird kid that eats paper or the know-it-all who could come or not come and still pass the tests.

You start doing mental calculations. You've planned a series of games and group activities that either A) can't be realistically modified for a single student or B) will involve you playing the part of another student and painfully trouncing poor paper-eater's feelings with your superior knowledge of English.

Then there's option C: just talking. Choose that option and you'll not only save paper-eater's feelings, but you'll also save yourself future work. Rather than playing catch-up with the missing students and remaking all the materials because you've already used them with this kid, you can just transplant your lesson to the following week. It's a freebie; it's just hella awkward.

It's uncomfortable enough to have forced conversations with strangers who speak your mother tongue. Just imagine doing that with someone who can hardly differentiate "was" and "were." It may seem hopeless, but consider this: you know those outdated *National Geographics* that clutter the tables of every waiting room in America? You're not a fan of them—no one is—but I guarantee you've looked at them.

Without finding anything interesting in your Twitter feed, you've sighed, put away your phone and started flipping through one. Those magazines are jam-packed with content. Even if "Stalking the Wild Ibis" or "Trekking the Tundra" haven't caught your fancy, I bet you've paused on articles like "Confessions of an Animal Dentist" or "Making Chocolate from

Fire Ants." Maybe you've even read through the whole thing and thought about it afterwards. It's not gripping entertainment, but it's not half bad either. Its weakness—and its greatest strength—are that it's all freely given.

You can't walk into a classroom conversation with the expectation of being politely listened to by your students. You'll be rudely interrupted either because your students don't understand you or because you're just plain boring. Shake it off. Keep in mind that you have a wealth of interesting experiences; not all of them will click with your audience, but the more you flip through, the closer you'll get to that one story that'll have everyone hooked.

I once sustained free conversation for two 70-minute classes with a low-level beginner ten-year-old. We leapfrogged from topic to topic: one minute it was robotic hands, the next minute it was video games, and even though that was a prime topic for us to discuss, we only spent about two to three minutes on each one. The conversation was essentially "look at this game. It's about such and such. I like/dislike it. Have you played it? Yes? No? Cool. Here's another."

I couldn't have done that five years ago. Part of being a sad sack is an inflated sense of self-importance. On one hand, you might feel an acute lack of interesting things to talk about and, therefore, place too much importance on protecting your scrawny ego. On the other, you might feel your wealth of experience is too sacred to be talked about with people unwilling to listen attentively to you. Tough. You're the same either way—a sad sack.

Why Yoda speaks the best English

Look at my handy-dandy table!	
General American English (GenAm)	[ˈwɑɾɚ]
Received Pronunciation (RP)	[ˈwɔːtə]
Cockney	[ˈwɔʔə]
Australian	[ˈwõɾə]
New York	[ˈwɔəɾə]
Irish	[ˈwɔθ̠ə]

How many ways can you pronounce the word "water?" If you're a General American English speaker, like me, then you'll probably say it with a back of the mouth "a", unrounded; the "t" will morph into a tap not unlike a "d"; and you'll keep the final "r" intact. If you're a Received Pronunciation speaker, you'll retain the "t", the "a" will be the same sound from "horse," slightly lengthened, but the final "r" will be dropped. If you're doing a more Cockney version, you'll drop the "t" for a glottal stop. If you're Australian, you'll keep the "horse" vowel, and omit the final "r", but the "t" will get the same treatment as it does in American English varieties. If you're from New York, you'll probably stretch that first vowel for all it's worth. If you're an Irish English speaker, you'll have a nifty little thing called a fricative "t" which doesn't fully block air flow during the production of the consonant.

Full disclosure: I'm making a shameless plug here for the International Phonetic Alphabet (which I, by the way, like very much and wish everyone knew), but I'm also making a point about how to say words. There's no monolithic "right" way to say a word. There are recommended ways to do it depending on context, teachers, goals, etc., but even so there's always room for variation. And this is just using a single, measly word as an example.

On that matter, there's one dude whose name you'll eventually run into—Adrian Underhill. He hosts conferences where he conducts choirs of teachers to belt out "uuuuuuuuuuugh," "euieu-ieuieui," "guuuuuuuugh" in unison as he swings a baton along a pronunciation chart. Take a look for yourself if you're curious:

https://www.youtube.com/watch?v=1kAPHyHd7Lo

In addition to giving us a dandy little chart, he also pitches a good, all-inclusive attitude to teaching pronunciation. Everyone ought to teach their students according to their own model of pronunciation. If you're a New Zealander, Canadian, Yankee, whatever, you just model your own patterns according to Underhill's chart and students reproduce it. It's almost too idealistic to be true.

And it is. Rarely will you find a school that will hire you if no one can understand you. Even if you come from a tiny, little island in the middle of god-knows-where and land a job teaching your mother tongue, the exoticism of your accent will force you to change because even giving simple instructions like "open your books to page 20" will be a challenge.

I can attest to this personally. The omission of "t" in "twenty" from my own dialect has caused so much confusion that at this point that I don't even say it naturally, opting instead for an exaggerated "TwenTy" where I'm hitting the "t" like it stole something.

A bloke from London who I used to work with had an even harder time with "th" because he pronounced it as either "v" or "f." He represented the, hands down, "REAL" London accent, but even words as simple as "the" or "father" caused communication problems for him. Thus he opted for an exaggerated posh accent where all the "ths" came intact.

On the flipside, it's not like you're gonna impose your own dialect on the students either—or at least not with much success. The Russians I worked with learned English based off an RP model, so they'll drop the "r" from the end of words, but getting them to produce the horse vowel is a real challenge. Every time I've led an Underhill style choir saying "coooooooooought" for "caught," they've always been like "nah" and gone with the more American style "a" sound. Curiously, though, they'll still produce the typical British "idear" instead of "idea," something which must've been drilled into them because it certainly doesn't make the pronunciation of the word any easier.

As much as you try and impose one way of speaking on a student, they'll drift away towards whatever's easiest for them. Hard to blame them, really. Who doesn't get sick of hearing their teacher say "no, but it's pronounced *softly, sooooooooooftly,*" all the while making faces at you and sticking out their tongue?

At the same time, you'll start drifting towards whatever's easiest for your students to understand. You'll expunge colloquialisms except for those few contextually obvious ones like "guys," "mate," "awesome," or "cheers." Your accent will flatten out into a sort of "international English" which maximizes intelligibility. Do it long enough and it may even stick. I had a brief stint at a hotel in my hometown—the very town where I had spent the majority of my life—and there was no shortage of guests who asked me where I was from. Some just thought I was Irish or Canadian, but there were a good number who thought I was "from some Slavic country."

Do it long enough and you may even wind up hating your own roots. An Aussie I worked with in Mexico once confided to me that he was sick of the Australian accent. He said that hearing it immediately made him cringe, that it just sounded uneducated to him now.

Anyhow, communication in the classroom is often a trade-off. Both the student and the teacher are constantly transitioning towards a universal brand of English. In pursuit of that, I'd argue that the most important things to teach are the differences that make a difference. Everything else can be regarded as adornments.

Take minimal pairs with /i/ and /ɪ/, for example—heat & hit, eat & it, bit & beat, fit & feet. There are like a gazillion different meanings you can make by swapping those two, so pushing for their differentiation is worth it. But then consider /ʊ/, the vowel from "book" or "foot;" if you swap that for the /u/ from "food", does it make a difference? Can you still understand it?

Not only with pronunciation, but also with words. We ought to weigh up the difference that one synonym makes over another. Russians have a thing for the word "serial." It's always "I watched a serial this weekend," "Netflix released a new serial yesterday." While I would personally say "series," I never bother to correct it. Likewise, if you've got a student who says "we had a bad problem with the car" or "we had a failure with the car," is the onus really on you to interrupt their perfectly intelligible story to say, "uhm, *actually*, it's 'the car *broke down*'" instead of letting them continue?

In every interaction we're like alpinists facing a mountain face we need to scale. Interacting successfully means you climb to the top, but you can only work with whatever tools you have at hand—be that bungee cords rather than ropes, paper clips instead of carabiners, or just your bare hands. You work with what you've got, and if that's enough, then way to go.

My administrator can't differentiate Thursday from Tuesday. In any conversation involving those days, it's always "we'll meet the day after Monday" or "on the fourth day of the week." You'd think that'd be an automatic deal-breaker for anyone whose *literal job* depended on scheduling, but no. On the contrary, I'd say she's the best boss I've ever had. She has never once failed to communicate a point to me or failed to receive my own. Maybe we beat around the bush a bit, but we always come to a satisfactory conclusion in the conversation.

In a world where we're spoiled for choice with all the varieties of English we can speak, why shouldn't we celebrate our diversity? A proficient second language learner will be one who harnesses the language as a tool to meet his/her ends. Even if it's something as simple as asking for directions to the swimming pool. The only real litmus test ought to be "Can I understand you?" After that, the diversity that speaker brings to the language ought to be accepted if not celebrated.

Learners of English often bring more to the language than we give them credit for. Consider the expression "long time no see." Has it ever struck you just how weird that construction is? It's a cobbled mess of adjective + noun + no + base verb. If I were to say "dirty shirts no wash," a la this formula, you'd peg me as a foreigner immediately; yet we don't think twice about it.

And, in fact, we owe that expression to Chinese immigrants from the West coast of the US. As so many language learners will, they spoke English by directly translating from their mother tongue. "Long time no see" was one such example. But it stuck—why? Most likely because it captured a meaning that English was deficient in expressing. We can just as easily say "I haven't seen you in a long time," sure, but why weigh ourselves down with the verbal baggage that the grammar imposes on us? Why not use something that expresses our appreciation directly? Grammar be damned, I'm happy to see you again.

It's the same situation with the expressions "so long," "no can do," and the underrated "you want I should...?" Not that every mistake a second language learner makes is automatically a poetic gem, but they could well become one.

If Yoda were a student, he'd be reprimanded fiercely for his jumbled sentence order, but Yoda's role is far from that of a student. He plays the master in all the Star Wars movies because he has something profound to communicate. He uses English effectively not only to communicate meaning, but even transcendently. He's harnessed and molded the language into something poetic, something that reflects his own goals in the words he uses.

Granted, Yoda is a fictional character. You can't use him as a singular example, but he does represent the spirit of those who harness English as an effective (if unconventional) tool. For a more modern example of this, look at Slavoj Žižek: a Slovenian philosopher is the farthest thing one could imagine from an internet celebrity, but this guy has garnered a respectable following. Vice News has gone so far as to label him "The Most Dangerous Philosopher in the West." It's jarring to listen to this guy speak—not so much because of the ideas he transmits, but just because of his accent. I dunno what he does with his throat, but there's some serious fricative action going on there.

For another example, I recommend watching *Exit Through the Gift Shop*. It's a documentary which, ostensibly, is about Banksy and his art. In reality, though, the star of the show is a Frenchman with an 19th century mustache called Mr. Brainwash who speaks more with gestures and facial expressions than words. He made the documentary because, in his words,

"I would make them live forever—those moments—y'know? Forever and ever. Making a documentary, it was like having the key of getting all these people. That's why I kept following them, following them, following them."

His sentence structures are irregular; he uses repetition as a crutch; he omits tenses in favor of just using the present while others only coexist in the company of verbs like "keep;" there's a glaringly obvious French accent to every word he pronounces; everything is peppered with "likes" and "y'know?" along with the occasional set phrase like "whatcha gonna do?" which just seems weirdly out of place. If I had to compare him to a food, I'd say he's like M&Ms on pizza—*weird*, really weird, yet surprisingly good. After all, how would he have hooked up with the likes of Banksy if he didn't know how to communicate effectively? This guy was privy to all the big names of the street art scene and at no point was he rejected because of his off-brand English. On the contrary, people seemed to like and even embrace him for it.

Get chumped or chump yourself

Do you know how <u>to make</u> a fire? I figure I could manage <u>to make</u> one if I had <u>to</u>. I mean, no one ever taught me how <u>to do</u> it in the classical sense of <u>making</u> one in the woods, but I get the gist of it: you go on <u>feeding</u> a little flame some sticks, leaves, paper and eventually the logs go on once it's big enough <u>to sustain</u> it-self. I think <u>starting</u> the flame would be the tricky part. I've seen people use a wedge of wood and a stick <u>to do</u> it, but I can't im-agine <u>doing</u> that myself. If I tried <u>to</u>, I guess I'd work it out, but I'm not about <u>to volunteer</u> for one of those wilderness survival shows. I'd end up <u>freezing</u> to death in the woods.

This is a fun conversation topic, by the way. With the exception of the pro-outdoorsy types, most of us have ONLY a vague sense of how to make a fire and we'll be more than happy <u>to swap</u> ideas about it. Bring it up at your next dinner party if you don't mind <u>being</u> forever known as "that one dude who wanted <u>to make</u> a fire in our dining room."

It's such a blast to discuss this, in fact, that I decided to use it for a class. We were working with this one book that was just relentlessly text heavy. Page after page was reading, reading, writing grammar, grammar, with only the occasional cartoon apologetically doodled into the margins; it was a conveyor belt of test preparation exercises whose only favor was organizing said exercises into thematic chapters—barely.

I hated it. The students hated it. So, naturally, I did my best to liven things up.

One day we were supposed to cover gerunds and infinitives (-ing and to- forms (see the underlined above for examples)). There was a mile-long list of uses for these things, but I figured it'd be better to set everything in a natural context: i.e. we'd talk about fires, especially how to make them. I'd jot down natural lan-guage that the students produced in context (much like above) and we'd all review it on the board. From there, it'd be a skip and a hop to the exercises.

More like a faceplant. The discussion about how to start a fire quickly became one about *what* and *why* I was so furtively writing on the whiteboard.

"But, Iain, why can't we say 'to build a fire is easy' rather than 'building a fire is easy?'"

Why indeed. If you've gone through public education, chances are you'll know that there's a short story by Jack London with exactly that title.

"Don't you worry! Just keep talking!"

"So, I can say to cook smores on the fire is nice?"

"Eh..."

From there things just disintegrated into discussions about nuance, complaints about nuance. It's a particularly frustrating point because it doesn't fit nicely into a table. No tidy little list of rules can be referred to. You just have to memorize everything on a case by case basis and always allow for exceptions (e.g. I would say "he admitted <u>to eating</u> the cake," but every book I've encountered lists it as "he admitted <u>eating</u> the cake"— which to me sounds like he was simultaneously stuffing cake in his mouth while confessing to some heinous crime) (there's another one: confess to + -ing) (guh).

Now, any sane English teacher here would've dismissed it all out of hand. "Well, I'm afraid that's just the way it works. English is weird like that" (nervous laugh), at which point the students would've figured "man, what a chump," but they would've also accepted it. He's a native speaker, after all. What he says must be true.

And, sure. I played the chump in that moment.

I was far from done, though. I was such a tool that I promised to research the topic in depth. I said we would review it all next class with a handy-dandy summary of the rules.

And who was gonna make that? The creators of our book who'd

already given extensive thought to the topic and organized the material in the most comprehensible way possible? No, no, no —I was convinced that *I* would find the pattern and create some bold new mnemonic or trick for mastering the great gerund/infinitive debacle.

But after a few hours of digging (even in etymological dictionaries because I liked blaming things on the French and suspected that loan words might be the culprits), I had pretty much nothing to show for my work. I cobbled together a table of rules as best as I could. My lesson plan for our next session was—eh—not too shabby, I guess, but there was no Grand Enlightenment. The students appreciated the attention to detail, but ultimately they just glanced at the table and said "ah." I was the only one to walk away from that class educated.

If, like me, you're a General American English speaker, I recommend the following scapegoats for similar situations:

A. **Blame it on the Brits**. If there's a bizarre word in a reading like "yobs," then chances are it's some Britishism. Even if it isn't, if your students have got you up against the wall, you can play it all off as just some quaint colloquialism.

(If you're an RP British speaker then you have no excuse as it's all your fault for making this language).

B. **Blame it on the French**. The incursions of French into English have wrecked the language much in the same way English is wrecking languages nowadays. Take pronunciation, for example; if not for the French, English would be like Icelandic—placing stress on the first syllable of every word. It still is, in some respects—as about 90% of words follow that pattern—but then there's the baggage of multisyllable romance words like "parasympathetic" or "concomitant," which most students will have no clue about. Is it paRAsympathetic? Is it concoMItant?

C. **Blame it on literary language.** If the students run across an idiom like "you've got egg on your face," which you're

76

kinda half aware of but still don't know how to use exactly, just dismiss it all with an "oh, no one uses that. It's just book language. Don't worry about it."

D. Blame it on the language itself. Saying "yeah, English is just weird like that" is an easy out; in fact, you can use it to disguise just about any level of incompetence or sloth on your part.

All these come with a caveat, though. By not having the answer to something which, ostensibly, you're an expert in, you make yourself a chump. The stereotype which most likely got you the job—the whole "only a *real* native speaker can give you the *real* language" thing—comes back to bite you. And for good reason—you are a chump.

The further you get into the teaching game, the less sense everything makes. Take tag questions, for example:

That was an aggressively adequate movie, <u>wasn't it?</u>
She's really dumb, <u>isn't she?</u>
You're not actually a doctor, <u>are you?</u>

It's pretty easy to deduce the rule to these and explain it: take the auxiliary verb (are, would, can, have, etc.) and make it either a negative or positive question. Was -> wasn't? Aren't -> are. No brainer.

At least until you run into this:

I'm a cool guy, <u>aren't I?</u>

Why, teacher? Why not "am I not?" Why not "amn't I?"

Why indeed. You certainly can't blame this one on the French, and it hardly seems to be the Brits' fault either. Guess you better play your "English is just weird like that" card and lose a little face.

Alternatively, you could spend a bunch of time researching trifles like this. You could learn the convoluted reasons behind English's greatest mysteries just to either (A) attempt to explain it to a bunch of students who didn't want an explanation in the first place and won't listen to it anyway, or (B) be ready for that one attentive student who will listen to you and then reply "ah... okay. That's pretty dumb, but I guess English is just weird like that."

Indeed, the reason behind that oddity is pretty dumb. The contraction of "am not" would naturally be "ain't" since "m" and "n" can't be pronounced together (or at least not in mainstream English). And "ain't" just ain't that popular, unfortunately. It's a real shame because it provides a handy negation of present auxiliary verbs regardless of the subject involved. Just look:

> It isn't gonna rain -> It ain't gonna rain
> We haven't eaten yet -> we ain't eaten yet
> I'm not happy about this -> I ain't happy about this

Due to its versatility, ain't may well become mainstream someday. For the moment, however, it's just a bit *too* handy. I'm damaging my image as a writer here just by using it, ain't I? People will peg me as a dumb try-hard, even if the alternative (aren't I?) isn't even correct in the first place.

The rules are only what we have until what's correct gives way to what's easy. And you, as a teacher, are here to play the hapless protagonist in this farce. You get paid for your part, which is something at least, but you're also the butt of every joke: every complaint about how the spelling of a word doesn't make sense, every misconjugation of a past tense verb, every nonsensical collocation—that's all on you.

And believe me, this isn't just abstract musing. When you've got a student who's an accomplished endocrinologist who worked in the States, published numerous research papers in English, and mainly speaks about sophisticated topics like Rembrandt's life and the works of Pushkin, you start to question whether you should bother correcting her for saying "we must to extend the trial period" or "they was amazed by the results." Heck, you're in an intermediate level class—she's learned this a million times over. Plus, she probably knows about these mistakes and just doesn't care. You can understand her. Maybe *you're* in the wrong for pushing a cruddy grammar system. She's got no grand ambitions with English, she comes here to let off steam mostly. Why not give her a space for safe rebellion?

There was a similar woman I once worked with in Japan. Her speech was riddled with grammar errors: stuff like missing articles, mixed up conjugations of the to be verb, and an aggressive use of the present tense for everything. There'd been teachers before me that tried correcting her and she simply wasn't having it. She complained so much that she even made one of them cry.

We, on the other hand, got on really well. I never tried to correct her. All I did was make her a transcript of the BBC's weekly news report with all the verbs removed, she'd fill them in as homework, then we'd check the answers together in class. Everything else was conversation about travel. She visited a new place practically every weekend and came back loaded down with souvenirs to share. A real worldly type, that one: she was a retired world history teacher who used to manage student exchanges and trips abroad. Maybe at some point in her globetrotting she came to realize that things like the preterite and the past participle had little relevance in the scope of human events.

Now. Obviously, I'm in no way saying that you should throw error correction to the wind. That's what you get paid for, after all. *You*, as the native speaker, are here to show everyone the proper way to speak. Play your role even if it's as the all too serious protagonist in a comedy who gets chumped by everyone. Be the chump you were meant to be. If you're lucky, you might even come to enjoy the jokes made at your expense.

Ground yourself in the CEFR

Back in Mexico, I once met a woman whom I can only describe as being a personified stalk of celery. I can't think of any other comparison that evokes the peculiar distaste she evoked. She emitted a cold and slightly limp quality in everything from her handshake to her demeanor. She welcomed me into her school with the same enthusiasm a half-off sale on potatoes would inspire. She stared apathetically into the corner as we talked, telling me about how her authority as a native English speaker was validated by her having been born in California—an authority I never challenged but nevertheless questioned as she continued mispronouncing words such as "stragedy" and "espert."

I had come to this woman's school on behalf of the exams department of our school. Every once in a while, we performed evaluations in some far-flung part of the state, but that particular day I was to be part of an elaborate ruse. Ms. Celery Stalk had it out for several members of her English teaching staff, but she couldn't just fire them flat out. Instead, she had to resort to a third party for the authority to say they were too incompetent to do their jobs.

What followed our lukewarm introduction was the interrogation of different teachers. We called them into a conference room where they sat across a heavy wooden table from us and hastily answered the celery woman's probing questions.

I was instructed to ask about teaching methodology, but my own innocuous questions about how teachers motivated students or how they taught grammar were overridden by my partner's coldly probing inquiries into qualifications, evidence of ongoing education, updated certificates. I assume conversations with the KGB went similarly to hers.

After each of our prisoners left, she turned to me for a final verdict. Needless to say, she wasn't impartial in her own judgments. She nitpicked how the teachers had spoken slowly, how they had pronounced "the" with a d sound rather than a th one, how they used the word "rabbit" instead of "bunny." In general, she held them to her own personal standard. She criticized them for not speaking like she did.

It doesn't take a petty person to fall into this trap. Without universal guidelines to judge students by, what can one use as a standard other than oneself? Ones parents and relatives? Actors and musicians from the media you've consumed throughout your life? Teachers? Motivational speakers? Neighbors? Friends? In short, all the people you already based your own speaking style off of? Even if you come from a place of good intentions, how do you justify your judgments as anything other than you saying "how much do you speak like me?"

There are many Englishes, and they extend far beyond what our sanctioned dialects of English prescribe. Take Indian English, for example: given its vast number of speakers, the attributes it's inherited from British English, the fact that it's become its own standard within the second most populous country on earth... doesn't that validate it as its own strain of whatever "real" English is supposed to be?

And that's just an obvious example. The point is that English is a tool that'll be used differently by everyone. It ought to be judged accordingly and, thankfully, we have a system in place to do just that, the wonderful Common European Framework.

According to that system, I ascribed a B2 level to every one of our interviewees, exactly what they needed for the job. Celery woman was less than pleased. She scoffed at me and demanded justifications. And that's exactly what I gave her: those teachers had shown an ability to use complex sentences with different tenses correctly. They had explored both familiar and unfamiliar topics with a good degree of spontaneity. They needed time to search for words or expressions, but not so much that it impeded conversation. When they didn't know a specific word, they expressed it through circumlocution. Moreover, the vocabulary they did utilize showed a good degree of specificity.

Their interaction was fluid and displayed good use of discourse markers. What pronunciation errors they did make were superficial as, overall, they were totally intelligible.

These are all factors (some among many) that go into determining one's CEFR level. The Common European Framework is one of the most sophisticated instruments a teacher can have at their disposal. If we're ever to overcome the celery stalks of the world, we need it. More importantly, we need it to avoid the pitfall of judging others for how much they do or don't speak like us.

An argument against the "ONLY ENGLISH" policy
Before going to Russia, my wife and I had a brief string of classes with different Russian teachers. The first was a Skype instructor who sent us meticulously crafted Word documents full of grammar rules; every class he'd thoroughly pick apart the nuances of how nominative nouns became plurals and voiced consonants became unvoiced in conjunction with consonant clusters and in terminal positions—all in Spanish. All told, we maybe exchanged a dozen words in Russian. There was no homework, no conversation practice. And, not surprisingly, he didn't last long with us.

Next, we took a two-week intensive course in Mexico City. The teacher was more to our liking because she used a real textbook and prompted us to *actually speak*, but we still came away from it disillusioned. The instructions were all in Spanish, as were the explanations. She made no effort to illustrate grammar, instead preferring to just explain it to us directly.

Likewise, my dad tried to hook me up with a private instructor in Denver, an old colleague of his. We met for lunch, he shook my hand, told me to sit down in Russian, launched into a windy explanation of how the verb was conjugated in the imperative according to number and formality, then shot off on a tangent about his teaching experience. The rest of the conversation was him reminiscing about his old teaching days at my dad's school.

When I asked him about material, he handed me a musty, old tome that would've been right at home in the library from *Harry Potter*; the cover unequivocally shouted "GRAMMAR" and the pages were crowded with a forest of tiny text explaining the many declinations of the word "chair." I didn't see him again.

The curse of being a professional is that you become a wet blanket for anything related to your field of work. Try watching an action movie with a demolitions expert or a martial artist, try having a bottle of cheap wine with a sommelier: in either case you're going to get an earful about how it's all wrong, everything, just everything's all wrong and we should feel bad if we like it.

Same case with teaching. I've had the ideals of this field hammered into me so much that now I hold everyone else to the same standards. My Japanese teacher in Russia, for example, was a total spaz who interrupted me at every turn, launched randomly into English, and prepared nothing else for the class than copies. A normal student would've probably admired him for his energy, found him charming. In my case, everything he did become an opportunity for me to think "I would've done it better." I wouldn't have interrupted my student with error correction, I would've taken careful notes and brought it up at the end of our conversation. I wouldn't just explain grammar by reading it off the page, I would've prepared a relatable context for the language and gone from there. Above all—I would've done it monolingually, even if it meant causing some confusion and slowing things down.

All tools and philosophies of the modern, effective English teacher. Everything else seems dated and barbaric by comparison. Yay for us—the enlightened.

You'd think. Let's hold one of those philosophies up for closer scrutiny, though. Namely, the "monolingual," "we only speak English here" approach. Cool: you reach an effective enough level of the language to say "I don't understand you" or "could you explain that to me?" At this point, you've got the bare bones for interacting in English and it can be justified to do it all monolingually.

Consider it from this angle, though. You're a 5-year-old kid. You can barely handle your own language, yet your parents have sent you to English lessons because "it's important for the future." You spend your time crying in the first few classes because it's an alien environment where the teacher makes strange noises you can't understand. You try to tell her "I'm scared," but she shushes you every time you say it. She shushes you whenever you say anything, in fact. She waves brightly colored objects at you while repeating more strange noises occasionally interspersed with games and songs. You just want to go home, but your parents won't have it. "Listen to the teacher," they tell you. "Do exactly what the teacher says," they tell you. Rather than interacting with this bizarre creature, though, you prefer to hide in the corner and weep some more.

Consider another case: you're a 14-year-old boy. You want to be a drummer, but instead of paying for drum lessons, your parents force you to go to English classes because "it's important for the future." You're cheesed off, so you never do your homework and never pay attention in class. You never asked to learn English, so you may as well make some friends while you're here. Every time you try to talk, though, this hairy ape of a teacher shushes you and assigns you extra homework. Even if you take the slightest interest in the class and ask questions about the material or ask for a translation, it's in your first language which —of course—this hairy ape doesn't speak. He shushes you again and you resolve to never try again.

Both of these cases are embarrassing examples of how the "English only" rule doesn't work. So embarrassing, in fact, that their culprits are quietly shuffled away into innocuous sounding "grammar classes" where everything is explained to them again in their first language so they can "catch up." And catch up they do because—wouldn't you know it?—speaking to a person in their own language is the best way to transmit information. You would almost think that it's a more effective way, in general, for people to learn.

These aren't outliers either. There's no shortage of apathetic teens or wailing children whose parents are pushing them to learn English. Moreover, for each of these groups there's no shortage of local language teachers who are willing to teach them—teachers who have thoroughly learned English through the same circumstances as their students and who—for bonus points—speak their language. Sounds pretty friggin' qualified, no?

But *you're* the native speaker! *You're* qualified by virtue of birth! *You're* qualified because you've got a certificate from some on-line class that you dumped 100 bucks on! Who but you could shepherd these students towards the true, one-and-only ENGLISH?

There's an interesting irony to all this. Maybe you've spotted it already. The "only speak in English" policy is almost axiomatic. Few people would disagree that a native speaker is the only one who can represent "real" English. That leads to the justification of English only classes as the "real" way to learn English. Coincidentally, the same teachers who espouse that philosophy are also the ones who can't speak the language of the students anyway. It'd be pretty unfortunate for their bottom line if suddenly people realized "hey, maybe my 5-year-old kid would be better off with a dude who can understand it when he says 'I'm scared' or 'I don't understand.' Maybe my misguided teen would be better off with a teacher who can tell him off in words he *actually* understands."

Mark my words: the second people get wise to this, we'll all be out of a job. The "SPEAK ENGLISH ONLY" argument is our last line of defense. Without it, people'll be quick to realize how incompetent we all are. For the moment, we can continue our awkward acrobatics of teaching without words (Lao Tsu would be so proud), but our days are numbered.

For that reason, be nice to your nonnative speaker coworkers. Despite them having funny pronunciations of certain words, despite them being underpaid and disrespected, they can teach circles around you. They're the ones who'll pick up the pieces of whatever mess we leave behind.

MATERIALS &
LESSON PLANS

When planning your lessons, think about the coastline of Great Britain

How long is it? Google it. Seriously. Look at a few different websites and you'll start to notice something odd. As of this writing, Brilliant says it's 11,072.76 miles; the CIA Factbook says it's 7,723 miles; and a dude from Stats, Maps n Pix has it calculated at 11,023 miles (but that's among several other numbers). Now, either everyone I've cited here sucks at math or there's a bigger factor at play.

You'll wind up with a different number depending on how you choose to measure the country. You could measure it from angle to angle, promontory to promontory, break it down into every bend and curve, or (if you're feeling particularly masochistic) measure it according to the distance from one grain of sand to the next. The more "exact" you get, the longer the coastline becomes. Take this to its (il)logical extreme and we could even say the coastline of Great Britain is infinite.

This same phenomenon can be applied to everything from snowflakes to trees. It's called the coastline paradox and, oddly enough, it can also be applied to lesson plans. If you broke down a lesson into its most stupidly rudimentary components, it would look like this:

1. Students come
2. Teacher teaches
3. Students leave

But that's pretty useless. If what you want from your plan is instruction, you'll obviously have to think about it in finer detail. So, let's try again:

1. Students come
    A. Check homework
2. Teacher teaches
    A. Cover pages 33 to 35
3. Students leave
    A. Assign homework: workbook page 28

Better, but still very limiting. There are some teachers who are comfortable working with just this, much to the chagrin of colleagues who cover their classes. Ideally, we should have something more helpful. Maybe something like this:

1. Students come
    A. Warm-up: pair discussion
    B. Check homework (WB pgs. 26-27)
2. Teacher teaches
    A. Cover pages 33-35
    - Present continuous introduction
    - Charades
    - Exercises at back of book
3. Students leave
    A. Assign homework: workbook page 28
    - Tell students to omit number 5. We'll do it tomorrow

Now we're getting somewhere. This plan is still far from perfect, but at least we know what we're covering in the class. What's more, we're starting to consider implementation: *how* exactly would we practice the present continuous?—with charades. *What if* the students can't do one of the exercises in the workbook?—we'll just do it together next class.

Perhaps you would have a lesson plan like this for an exam day. It's not unthinkable. After all, the students come, they take the exam, then they leave, no? It's probably the simplest part of the whole job.

Or so it would seem. In reality, even on the simplest day you run the risk of hitting an unforeseen snag. I can attest to this as, even now, I've not developed a perfect way to coordinate exam days. They are, in my opinion, the days which lay bare a teachers' worst planning flaws.

For example, it's a no-brainer that you should separate students to avoid answer sharing. Sure, but how do you prevent people from talking across the row or talking to the person behind them, especially in a classroom with limited space? You could seat students next to whomever they're least likely to talk with, but then you'll have to map out the classroom according to available space and friendship hierarchies within the class.

Then imagine if, after all that, you suddenly discover you've got the wrong exam. One particular time, I started a listening, sat down in my chair with a good book, and then was rudely interrupted by an "um, teacher?"

As it turned out, the recording was a British man blathering about snow leopards, but the questions were all about the history of carrots. Other times the recording didn't even work. Other times we didn't have enough copies for all the students. Other times the questions were a complete nightmare or were just blatantly wrong.

I could go on and on. The reason I bring up exam days is because they illustrate that implementation—and, by extension, preparation—is key. People outside academia assume we just "wing it"—we open our books, read the grammar descriptions, and then the students do exercises. And, yeah, there are teachers like that—but they're the bad ones. They put little to no thought into how their actions impact the students.

That said, let's go back to our lesson plan. Specifically, let's take a closer look at the warm-up:

    A. Warm-up: students discuss morning routines
    - Teacher greets students
    - Teacher reads warm-up questions to students
    - Teacher breaks students into pairs
    - Pairs discuss questions
    - Pairs report back to class

Nice. This offers a great outline for all the little details involved with the activity. Pedantic as it may sound, even something as obvious as the teacher reading the questions to the students may be crucial: imagine if you included a word that none of the students knew like "morning smoothie," their looks of confusion on hearing that word would give you an opportunity to teach the word. Otherwise, they might wind up talking about something totally unrelated, getting the wrong idea about what exactly a smoothie is, ending early, or spending five minutes on their phone trying to translate "smoothie" and consequently giving you the impression that they were goofing off. Plan out the steps and you'll avoid such hang-ups.

How specific do you really need to get, though? Shouldn't there be times on the lesson plan? Shouldn't we include the questions we're going to write? Should we instead write them on pieces of paper? Should we include a note about what we're checking for like correct use of present simple or adverbs of time?

The answer to all of this depends on the group. If you've got a sharp group of students, chances are they won't need any hand-holding; a pack of adrenaline-charged teenagers, on the other hand, are a catastrophe just waiting to happen.

Depending on the composition of the class, even the slightest misstep can ripple to disastrous proportions. Class size, for instance, can make a world of difference. One time I took some colored balls to class with the intention of practicing prepositions of place (e.g. the red ball is between the blue and yellow ball, etc.). What I didn't consider, though, was how difficult it'd be to give specific directions by myself to a room full of 25 rambunctious high schoolers.

The second the balls came out, any hope of getting their attention was totally lost. It was a complete circus. Like, literally —there were people juggling balls at the back of the classroom like circus clowns. They were so popular that the only way I could regain control was by forcing them out into the hall. To date, I still remember that as one of my worst classes.

Like a ship circumnavigating the coast of Great Britain, you won't need to know how many trees are on every island or whether there's a coffee shop in the first town you pass, but you will need to know what's in your path. Some classes are icy land masses surrounded by drifting icebergs. Others are like the smooth, curvaceous Caribbean islands we see in tourism posters.

Not every class will be smooth sailing (and it'd be prudent to approach them all like this to begin with), but eventually you'll know which ones have rocks in the shallows. At that point, you'll develop your own style of lesson plans to chart a course. In my case, a lesson plan at its most and least detailed looked like the following examples, respectively.

There's a general structure I use for all my plans: materials at the top with the class name and date, lesson aims on the right, and a sequence of events from most general to most specific that goes number -> letter ->dash -> dot. Depending on how granular I have to get, I can telescope that sequence into even including the physical actions necessary for setting up an activity. E.g. write this first, hand this out second.

There are people—most often observers and coordinators—who will expect you to do this for every lesson plan you write. Those people are idiots. Take note: if you do this, you will spend twice or three times the length of the class on planning. Eventually you won't have time to eat or sleep.

I've never gone into a class *without* a lesson plan, but when I know what to expect from a group, I usually just jot it down on a scrap of paper. The idea is to know what's gonna happen, why, in what order, and what you'll need for it. As long as you've got that, you're set.

15/11 Sol. 2 | HAVE: •Qs on WB •Book audio •Projector
•Identity parade pairs on walls •Kahoot
•Grammar rule cards •Comparison cards

0. Check HW: WB pg. 30   5:00 - 5:05

1. Comparatives & Superlatives Review (pg. 35)
   a. Lead-In: 5:05 - :20
      - Ss discuss the following Qs with a partner
        • What's the best/worst film genre?
        • which is better: fantasy or sci-fi?
        • which is worse: romance or musicals?
        • what's the most interesting film you've ever seen?
        • what's the dullest film you've ever seen?
      - Underline indicated words, elicit comparatives + superlatives then write on WB
   b. Practice: 5:20 - :40
      - Ss complete grammar box
      - Ss complete # 4 together
      - MWB race (pg. 110) # 2
   c. Production: 5:40 - :6:00
      - Ss complete #3 (pg. 110)
      - Runner/writer: Comparisons race

TRANSITION: Set context for listening — "I'm shooting a romantic film. Who should I hire for the lead role?"

2. As/Too/Enough (pg. 37)
   a. Presentation: 6:00 - :15
      - (Books CLOSED) Ss listen to find who the casting directors hired — Carrie or Sheila
      - (Books OPEN) Ss read and answer Qs — Elicit structures by asking for rationale.
      - Ss paste grammar rule cards to WB (see back)
      - CCQ by repeating casting activity
   b. Practice: 6:15 - :30
      - #s 11 + 5 in book
      - Kahoot
   c. Production: Debate with comparison cards
                  (which thing is better?) ← (IF TIME)

HW: WB pgs. 31 & 33 ; SB pg. 36 #s 2+3

LO1: To review comparative structures
LO2: To make visual, demand and equivalence comparisons with as/too/enough

27/5 FF3 Ⓐ | HAVE: •Timer
•Scr. Sn •SBaudio
•Cards + cube
-Postcards

0. Timed throws

Check HW: WB 100-101
SB 73
Scr.
Sentences

1. Going to (pgs. 110, 112)
a. FC games
b. Song
c. Q + A
  - Model Q + A w/ #1
  - Question line
d. Reading
  - Do Qs
  - Model for postcard
    activity
  - Postcards

HW: WB 102 + 104

LO2: To review and reinforce "going to" for plans

The forbidden love of paper

I figure paper is the best unit for measuring languages. Nuts to proficiency exams and report cards, if I ever hire a translator, I want to know how much deforestation their education has caused.

Just as a teacher I must've killed an entire redwood by this point. There are the obvious culprits like books and notebooks, sure, but mostly I place the blame with copies.

I once gave an FCE (First Certificate of English) preparation course to a class of 15-some students—not one of whom had a book. Each class was about three-and-a-half hours and each page occupied about 10 to 15 minutes, so you can just imagine the stacks of papers I was lugging around. The worst part was that I sometimes got the wrong page or forgot to make enough copies for everyone or just fudged a copy altogether. That sent me running up and down the stairs in the middle of class to fetch that final copy from our school's only photocopier. Never mind that some days the cartridge ran dry or there was no paper left.

That would've been all well and fine for the first class (protip: a lot of courses will launch before all the students have the book, so come prepared with copies), but it didn't end there. We didn't all get our books until about the third or fourth week. Even I didn't have one. I needed to swipe my colleague's book for copies. The lady at the bookshop wasn't helpful either. Every time I stopped by, it was always "they're *suuuuuuuuper out, teacher. Suuuuuuuuper out.*"

The madness of copies goes beyond just books, though. If I go into the classroom without some extra worksheet or cut-up text to use, I don't last long. Try burning through all the activities a textbook suggests (even the last-minute corner-fillers like "make a poster about the nutritional benefits of bread") and you'll only fill about half the class.

No matter how tightly you plan your class in paper, though, you wind up hemorrhaging it everywhere. Whether it's because a student didn't come or we got sidetracked talking about weird buskers on the train, I always end up with more copies than I know what to do with. (I used to think it was just me, but at this point I've seen enough of my colleagues' bulging course folders to know better).

And why not? Paper has a talismanic quality. Going into the classroom with a neatly clipped stack of worksheets and board-games is like having a magical forcefield around you. Maybe the book will fail you, maybe the students won't take to the topic or will know the grammar point already, but you've got backup. Those pages can be the only thing between you and a 30-minute lull where the children stare you down with knowing eyes, smelling the fear of unpreparedness wafting off your brow.

We had a part-timer back in Russia who learned this the hard way. She was hired as a first language teacher to give supplementary lessons to students who just weren't cutting it. She knew her rammarg backwards and forwards, even more so than the normal teachers, but she got the rug pulled out from under her the first time she taught one of my groups. The topic was will & going to—enough to fill a class by itself, but she went into it expecting a lecture.

Big mistake: in about 15 minutes she'd run through her elegantly simplified explanations, wrote things on the board in well color-coded columns, and rather than turning around to a class of attentive students with insightful questions, was blasted with a chorus of "but we know! We know!" (They always lie about that). Her eloquent explanations disregarded, the exercises in the book already finished in sloppy scrawls, what was there left to do for the hour of class that remained?

After that, she was never caught unprepared again. We could always tell when she had a class for the day because she spent a good 20 minutes copying grammar pages in the teachers' room. Half of them wound up on our desks afterwards, unused. And if we wanted more (which we didn't), she was never shy about her source material; pretty much every conversation with her was some variation of "I found such and such exercise in such and such shop or on such and such website."

Paper is the lifeblood of language classes. Despite that, it occupies an almost taboo place in the language conversation. No one advertises their school as "a place where a native speaker will give you worksheets!" and for good reason. It's just not sexy enough to make sales. There's an emphasis on conversation and the oral method, but that can only take you so far. Unless they're adults, many students simply won't talk without prodding or reverting to their first language. Even if they are inclined to talk, anyone with a B1 level or lower will start losing steam within a few minutes. Then there's class size: you, as a teacher, can painfully struggle through a one-on-one conversation with a single student, but try doing the same with a class of 15. Faced with these limitations, what do you turn to?

Try doing a listening—you'll need paper for the questions. Do surveys or interviews—paper for the answers. Watch a video and discuss it—you'll need a paper with instructions on what to take notes about. Read and discuss a text—paper.

In our continual efforts to surrender our lives to computers, schools have tried turning to the paperless mecca of a "digital classroom." I witnessed this firsthand as one of my schools transitioned from using a single textbook/workbook format to an online platform. Students were instructed to buy the traditional books, register on the platform using a code from page whatever, the teacher would dispense prepared homework assignments for everyone and prompt discussions in the forum, the final grade would be a composite of all the work done online, then everyone would clap their hands and sing "Kumbaya."

Can you guess what happened? Cuz it certainly wasn't that. Teachers and students only half-heartedly used the platform or just ignored it outright. Some students didn't even bother registering or couldn't because of compatibility problems. I recall spending an entire class getting 25 different students to register on their phones and only having about a 50% success rate because of varying obstacles. The phones just wouldn't connect to the internet, the password or code were rejected, they couldn't find the right classroom to sign into, or—most frequently—they hadn't even bought the book; they came to class expecting what traditional classrooms have always promised: a teacher who acts as the sole gatekeeper of knowledge and vomits it all out in waves of paper.

Paper, paper, paper. It's an inescapable evil that we're loathe to acknowledge. Schools will try in vain to hamper the raging avalanche with printer restrictions. Textbook companies will speak of copies as if they were Voldemort. My wife once helped write a textbook and in a presentation made the fatal mistake of uttering such a blasphemy. After showing off all the bells and whistles it featured, a teacher asked her "what do we do if the students don't have the book" (a common problem, after all), to which she replied "well, you can make copies." Her coworker gave her a dressing-down for that: "you *don't* mention copies. They *don't* exist. It's *all* about the product."

There was an episode of the podcast Flash Forward in which they interviewed a representative from a paper company about the possibility of a paper-free future. Without even a second thought, he shot down the idea. He pointed out that paper use has, ironically, gone up with the digital revolution, not down. I'm not gonna quote you an exact figure for it here, but if you want I'll gladly take a picture of my scrap bin for you as evidence.

In a far-off future with flying cars and underwater cities, more enlightened folk will look back on our paper-crazed society as barbaric, I guess. Personally, I'm not holding my breath, and neither should you. Be optimistic if you want, but stick to what works.

One of the things I highlight as an accomplishment of my time as a teacher was the establishment of a digital test bank for my entire school. At the end of every course, it used to be the co-ordinator's job to crank out hundreds of tests for every teacher in the school all by herself while simultaneously juggling placement exams and just general bureaucratic pencil pushing. It was madness. Tests often arrived late, with defects, they were the wrong one, or somehow we were accidentally given a page from the *Necronomicon.* In short, we always had to pick up the slack ourselves on the very same day of the final exam.

In response to this, I spent several weeks encrypting and arch-iving all the tests from the main computer into a shared Google Drive. All the administrator had to do was give us the access codes and we could print the exams ourselves—instant access to the PDFs and MP3s for everyone, no fumbling around with audio CDs or mixing up botched exams. At first it seemed like a grand success. One year down the line, though, the system had reverted; the teachers took no initiative to ask for codes and the administrator became what she always was—a gatekeeper to the sacrosanct realm of paper, the great printer in the sky.

99% of what you're looking for already exists

Textbooks are weirdly paradoxical. You'd be hard pressed to teach a class without one—and, believe me, I've tried; every hour of class took me three hours of preparation. But then, once everyone's finally got the books, you suddenly find yourself hard-pressed to use it effectively. The material in it is almost always insufficient.

Your lesson will invariably be based off whatever comes next in the textbook. At that moment you'll be picking your brain for some way to pad out the book's meager material. Say you're teaching the present continuous and the theme is exercise: there'll be a few pictures of people riding bikes, swimming, and playing soccer plus some fill-in-the-blank sentences. In the middle of all that, like a polar bear scrambling around on a melting chunk of ice, there'll be a grammar box that no one reads. Look to the back of the book and you'll find some linear notes about what the present continuous is. No one will read that either. You'll have a workbook too, but that'll be saved for homework.

You're not gonna fill an hour and a half with that.

So? What do you do? You get extra materials. That begs the inevitable questions of where, how, and how long it will take. You might be tempted to make those materials yourself, but always remember this—they'll suck. Whatever you've got in mind, someone's already done it better—with nicely trimmed backgrounds, drawings, custom fonts, and carefully thought out exercises. It exists. You just need to know where to look for it.

Chances are you'll start online—and you'd be right to do so. Google "INSERT GRAMMAR POINT HERE worksheet" and bam. You'll be inundated in sites clamoring for your attention—most of them pretty shoddy ones too. Rather than shop around, it's best to find one or two reliable sites. Personally, I recommend ISL Collective. Their documents are haunted by the hollow-eyed ghosts of clip art children, but they're thorough and dense; just one of them can eat up a good 15 to 20 minutes and run you through the most exhaustive of grammar contortions (e.g. "France has been gone to BY ME," "a piano is being played BY ME").

Don't stop here, though, because an even greater treasure trove lies forgotten in the jumbled bookshelves and cramped storage closets of most schools—the world of photocopiable materials.

Pretty much every English textbook is the same at heart. The only thing that changes are the fonts, inclusion of color, and replacement of dead or morally tainted celebrities with Justin Beiber. After that, administrators take the old books and stuff them into the unloved corners of the school. Flip through these resource books and you'll find surveys, lovingly rendered drawings, boardgames, and all manner of delightful materials that'll give your lessons a thoughtful, dedicated touch.

Moreover, don't forget to check your main textbooks for extra resources. Usually there's a section at the back of the teacher's book, on a website, or on an accompanying CD that's crammed full of PDFs to fling at your jaded pupils.

For example:

You have a very large nose and try to cover it up by wearing your hair over your face, but you are becoming increasingly sensitive about it.

No one ever wants to work with you in meetings. You are worried it could be a problem of bad breath.

You are a young woman with very large breasts. Every time you meet a new man he never takes into account the fact that you are very intelligent.

Despite being from a ten-year old textbook, these scenario cards are gold for any topic related to advice. I remember I once had a business English class where we were studying something related to job hunting. After the mechanical listenin-greadthedialogueanswerthequestionsredothedialoguefrom-memory, I brought these things out and everyone immediately perked up. I always made sure to give the well-endowed woman card to a guy too. That was good for a few laughs.

If not for me, though, these cards would've languished in my school's backroom. Teachers and administrators overlook old materials as incompatible with whatever newfangled textbook they've just bought, but that couldn't be further from the truth.

Have another example. The following cards are from a kids' book that's also about ten-years old at this point. The original idea was for the students—who had just learned how to use "may" for predictions—to look at the pictures and say "he may be die," "he may be kill" (because, honestly, they always resort to those verbs, predictable little snots that they are).

It's not like we stop making predictions after "may," though. On the contrary, predictions reappear in a motley of forms throughout textbooks. Just look: "he could die," "he might well die," "I feel he will die," "I expect him to die," "he'll probably die," "if those eyes had been monsters, he probably would've died." Why would you deny students the joy of making progressively more advanced predictions about fatalities just because the resources involved were a little old or originally intended for children?

This becomes doubly frustrating when you consider the nature of the job. You *need* supplemental materials for class. There's no way around that. If there was, why would textbook companies continue making these resource packs?

And yet, they do. Meanwhile, perfectly good resources gather mildew in a closet and teachers who don't know better spend untold extra hours making their own materials.

Don't do that. 99% of the time, whatever you need already exists; it's just a question of finding it. For that other 1% of the time, take pride in creating something truly original.

For example:

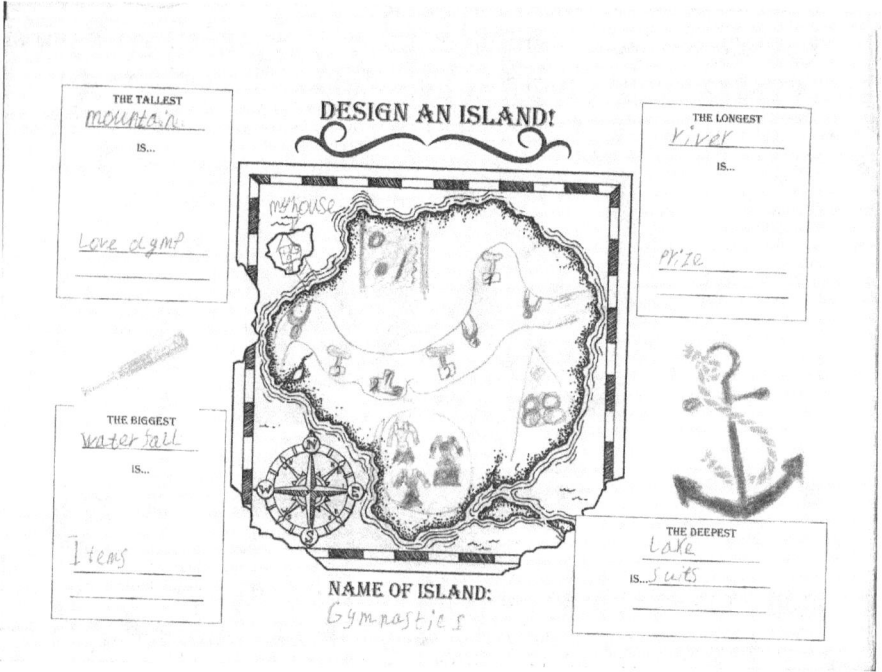

I cobbled this thing together in about 5 minutes from Google Images clip art, but I couldn't be prouder of it. It's so basic that I've been able to repurpose it many, many times. Relative clauses?—write a description of the things on the island. Geography?—name and describe the features of the island. Writing a tourist brochure?—write a description of your own, original island. Superlatives?—write what the tallest, deepest, longest etc. on your island is.

The results have been nothing short of amazing. I mean, just look at this thing: the deepest lake is suits. What is that even?

More than that, though, what pleases me about it is the labor saved: less work for more results. That ought to be what every supplementary material does for a teacher.

Variations on a Theme

A coworker of mine once said that working with small children is like working with dogs. You can spend untold hours making them fetch a ball and it will *never* get old for them. Even better, you can pretend to throw the ball, hide it under your armpit, and once they've looked for it everywhere in vain, you can pop it onto the desk and say "wow! It was there all along!" They'll figure it out eventually, but it's surprising how long you can keep up the charade.

In reality, just about everything with them can be repeated ad nauseum. Teach them to play bingo once and they'll insist on playing it every class. Show them how hangman works (I'm not allowed to play that game, by the way—parents have complained it's too morbid) and they'll always ask for it—even if it's just to practice mundane vocabulary. I once taught my kids how to play Go Fish for practicing questions and answers and now they want to play it every class (never mind that the cards were just sloppily scissored rectangles I got off the internet which I had to write color names on because the printer only did black-and-white copies).

This is what makes classes with kids the easiest to prepare; every lesson plan is essentially just a list of games with slight notes about variation and order. You'd think that wouldn't be the case with older students, but I'd argue that the pattern actually continues throughout our development, it just takes on more sophisticated forms.

Take the "where's your ghost?" activity, for example. It's pretty straightforward: first you give everyone a diagram of the rooms of a house and you make sure everyone knows basic furniture vocab. From there, everyone "hides" their ghost somewhere and the other students have to guess where it is by asking questions like "is your ghost under the fridge? Is it above the sofa? In the sink?"

I've seen this game go off without a hitch for the oldest of adults and the youngest of kids. It never fails to entertain. Likewise, let no one tell you that adults don't enjoy throwing balls at each other or making idiots of themselves with charades. Whether it's stuffing a ghost in a piano or pretending to be a pelican, these are integral parts of a pattern that continues throughout our lives and language levels. Hack that pattern and you'll be Neo out of *The Matrix* seeing all those spaghettish strands of code dribbling down from the ceiling.

This is why I always told my coordinator "forget the droning theory lectures! We need workshops about ways to reformat readings! About how to gamify vocabulary lists and grammar items!" No one needs to know the developmental stages of a child according to Piaget. You figure that out yourself through common sense and experimenting. What we really need is a lesson on how to spruce up normal lessons with variations.

No one's gonna listen to me there, though. Somehow "gamify a vocab list" doesn't come across as a respectable name for a workshop. Whatever. For what it's worth I'm gonna share some strategies for variations here that'll serve you well for those times when the book just sucks (which it will—a lot).

1. <u>Vocabulary</u>

Here's an example list of words about transport that you could encounter in any textbook: train, tram, motorbike, car, plane, helicopter, ship, bike…

If you stick purely to the book, you'll wind up doing a match the picture to the word exercise and maybe a fill-in-the-blank exercise afterwards. That'll take five to ten minutes. With that, even the most attentive student will only remember a handful of the words for lack of using them. So, what do you do?

- **Write the word race:** this one's pretty self-explanatory. You (or one of the students) gives hints about one of the words (e.g. "it's big, it's in the water") and then the students have to write the corresponding word. There are two good variations for this: the first is a run to the board type—sort the students into lines facing the board with markers in hand, shout "go!" after the hints, and they'll have to run and write the word for points; the second necessitates mini-white boards (I can't emphasize how handy those are, by the way, so I recommend buying a bunch of them for your classes) —it's the same, just that the students have to write the word without running. The first type is good for younger kids; the second is good for just about everyone.

- **Complete the sentence race:** using the same materials (especially the mini-white boards (BUY THEM)), slap together a simple PowerPoint with either a fill in the blank sentence, a definition, a sentence with an error, etc. and have the students compete to rewrite it correctly.
- **Run to the wall:** especially good with little kids or teens. Write the vocab words on the walls, shout out your hints, and the first student to run and smack the correct word gets a point. Beware, this game is potentially hazardous (I once nearly brained a kid with an air conditioner doing it), so you can have the learners chuck plush toys or balls at the words if you're wary of injuries.
- **Headbandz:** get some sticky notes. Write the words on them. Slap them on the students' heads and have them guess what the word is based off a partner's hints. The sticky notes are purely for gimmick value (in reality, you can use simple scraps of paper pulled from a hat or even just trust students to pick words from the book themselves), but sometimes the gimmick value is worth it.
- **Bingo:** not the dog. Also: don't waste your time making bingo cards beforehand. Have your students make their own from scrap paper and a list of vocab words either from the book or the board.

- **Word scramble:** do this as a warmup while you check homework or wait for everyone to arrive. Write a jumble of letters on the board, give the students markers, and have them decode what the words are.
- **Mindmap:** do this before giving vocabulary to set the theme and preteach the meanings of more difficult words. Draw a circle on the board with the vocabulary theme in it (e.g. "transportation") and have everyone connect related vocab to it.
- **Charades:** I'm silently doing gestures to demonstrate what this is, you just can't see me.
- **Spider:** this is the same as hangman, but instead of lynching someone you pull the legs off a spider one-by-one. Our school finds it less morbid. Go figure.
- **Memory:** you already know what this is (weirdly it's also called Pelmanism). Write the words on cards or whatever, put them face down, show them, students have to remember which is which, and so on.
- **Boardgames:** if you don't know what a boardgame is, I pity you. Prep a good stock of blank boardgame templates on your computer and you can repurpose just about anything. You're only limited by your own creativity here, but I personally recommend the standard roll the die and move around the board style of game with instructions written in each square.
- **Crosswords:** likewise. Grab crosswords from any generator on the web and chuck them out like ninja stars. They have the added advantage of being useful after and before the vocab is introduced. E.g. if you have students who don't pay attention to definitions in the book, force them to do a crossword instead and they'll have to read whatever word it is that they're perfunctorily slapping into the answers).
- **Shiritori:** you say "elephant," I say "turtle," the next person says "egg," "grandma," and so on. People contribute words to the chain, the first letter of each

one being the last of the previous one, until someone can't. Incorporate a theme or a timer to make it more dynamic.

- **Slap:** this game requires flashcards (get PDFs of as many of those as you can before you start working because they are insanely useful). Put everyone around a table, call out a word that corresponds with one of the cards, and the first student to hit the card gets a point. You can regulate this yourself or break the students into groups and designate someone as "the dealer" to provide cards to the others.

- **Slow reveal/run and grab/jump/shout:** did I mention flashcards are insanely useful? All of these are games you can play with them. For the first, slowly show the card until someone shouts it correctly; for the second, stick the cards around the room and have the students run and grab the correct one; for the last two (which are more appropriate for younger learners) students have to either jump or shout a word at a certain volume when a card appears.

2. Grammar:

- **Sentence generator:** have you ever noticed that there are six subjects and objects in English? Probably not, but you know what you have noticed that has six parts? A die. (whoa!) Get a little plastic cube, write the subjects or objects (He, she, you, we, they, I...) on it, toss it on the floor, and have the students make a sentence accordingly. For more variation, you can include a coin to determine negative and positive, incorporate flashcards, use a spinner to incorporate tenses, etc. It's especially helpful in the early stages of English because the whole does/doesn't/didn't, he runs/I run, I am/you are/she is thing is a pain to explain to people who don't even know the words for subject or verb.

- **Writer/Runner:** this can also be called running dictation, but I find my name more evocative. Before class, write some scrambled sentences on scraps of paper. Say you're teaching the irregular past simple—you'd have various slips of paper around the room saying "run/not/she/yesterday" and the sentence would have to come out as "she didn't run yesterday." Peg all this up on walls around the classroom and have students race in pairs to unscramble each one. The key is to do this activity in pairs—one student writes the answers while sitting, one student runs and dictates. You can easily mug up your sentences on a Power-Point slide—5 minutes of effort for a 15-minute activity that gets everyone moving.

- **Kahoot:** you know how a snake charmer can hypnotize a snake into dancing out of a basket with a flute? That's what this website does for students (https://kahoot.com/). I dunno what it is, but some combination of the bright colors and bouncy music mesmerizes them. At no point do they realize that it's just a dressed-up version of a worksheet. Like, literally, I've copied the exact same multiple-choice questions from a worksheet onto this and they went crazy for it. It's hard to do it justice in words here, though, check it out for yourself and use it at your own risk; once the genie's out of the bottle, there's no getting it back in.

SHIRITORI:

TRAMPOLIN**E**

ENTREPRENEU**R**

RUGBUR**N**....

Can	___	A	Milk	Sugar	Need	?	You
Have	I	?		How	Do	___	
___	People	Didn't	See	Isn't	There	Energy	For
I	On	Train	That	On	Everyone	___	Earth
Money	___	To	I	My life	Difficult	Is	Have
Buy	It	Have	Don't	I		___	Problems
People	Aren't	___	In	I	Have	___	Only
There	Fa						

Make a template box in word or PowerPoint and fill it with scrambled sentences. Cut and peg them on the walls to play Writer/Runner

NB: the blanks are optional, but provide good variety

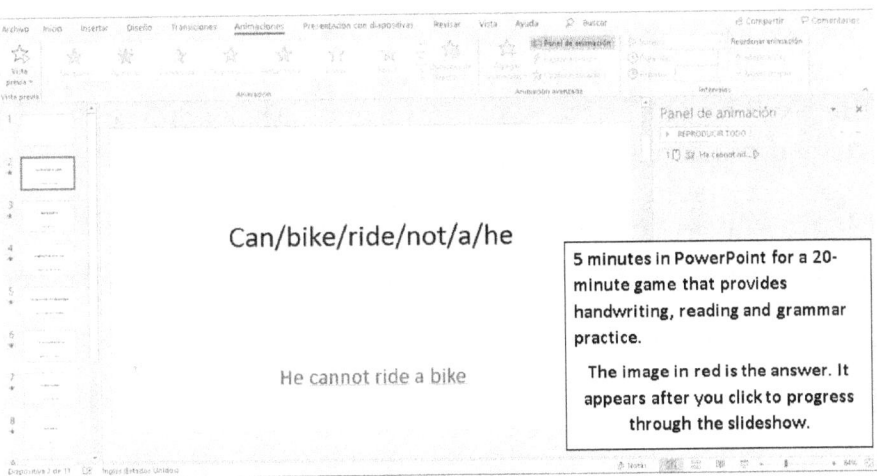

Can/bike/ride/not/a/he

He cannot ride a bike

5 minutes in PowerPoint for a 20-minute game that provides handwriting, reading and grammar practice.

The image in red is the answer. It appears after you click to progress through the slideshow.

Any of these activities can be repurposed for grammar or vocabulary, mind you, but they tend to be most useful as I've organized them here. "Repurposing," in fact, is the keyword here. One of the things I like most about teaching is the opportunity for creativity it offers. Every new page in the textbook is its own engineering challenge—how to present the context, whether to separate it from or further entwine it with the target language, what patterns of interaction to implement, what section to start and finish with, even how to arrange the desks. No two classes are exactly the same because everything has to be repurposed. What I've presented here is just a selection of the more consistent elements of an ever-evolving pattern.

Evan Hadfield has a great video about a bunch of rocks off the coast of Canada. As he admits from the get-go, they're just that —unassuming rocks—but as they contain secrets to the origin of life they're just as important as they are boring. At Mistaken Point there are fossils of a unique and no longer extant type of life: fractal organisms. They're called fractal organisms because they're a larger version of their smaller selves. In Evan's words, it would be like a horse made out of smaller horses; take out your microscope to look at it and it'd be "horses all the way down."

Why don't they exist anymore, though? Because the time of fractals gave way to more complex, less symmetrical forms of life. Even so, the critters that followed in the Cambrian Period were just another building block in the complexity of biology, another twist in the pattern. Likewise, with classes going up the ladder of age and level, things remain as much the same as they become newer and more complicated. Hack the pattern and you'll have a blueprint for any student, any class.

The monotony hammer

Y'know how we're all supposed to have a learning style? Like: you're an audio-visual learner so you learn best by just watching TV and never opening a book, you're an emotional-visual-musical learner so you learn best by watching people cry and then emulating them to a hip-hop beat?

Yeah, it's all bunk.

Don't get me wrong, people have preferences, and that's precisely the keyword—*preferences*. I, personally, prefer to learn language through books; I buy a kids' book when I'm learning a new language and tediously trudge through the blocks of new words with a dictionary app open on my phone. Some people prefer to just jump into conversation with whatever limited vocabulary they have and ad-lib it because the spoken aspect of language is the most important thing to them. You could say those people are verbal learners. You could say I'm a visual learner because I prefer to see things written down. But, once again, the keyword here is "prefer."

But don't take it from me. You can find numerous studies online debunking the bunk which is learning styles. You can even get the condensed version here in this Ted-talk:

https://www.youtube.com/watch?v=855Now8h5Rs

Beyond empirical evidence, just consider the impracticality of learning styles. Let's say you've got a kid who's a "kinesthetic" learner. How on earth are you supposed to teach him "kinesthetically?" For a few topics with real world references, you can do it (e.g. body parts—Simon says; verbs of action—listen and do); once the first grammar point comes up, though, you're pretty much jacked. Are you gonna transform the differences between will and going to into textures that he'll interpret while wearing a blindfold? Are you gonna find a song that he can dance to for every lexical set under the sun and then somehow translate that into the textual knowledge of spelling necessary for a test?

Even so, schools will stress the importance of learning styles. At any given teacher training session, at any given conference, the topic'll be brought up with an air of unassailable authority. Whenever you have an observation, chances are the rubric'll have a column labeled "RECOGNITION OF LEARNERS' LEARNING STYLES" and you won't get full marks for it unless everyone is dancing, singing, and flying around the classroom.

Again: preference. As the woman from the TED Talk says, we persist in our beliefs about learning styles because they give us a comfortable sense of self. I can write off conversation as infeasible for me because I'm a visual learner (rather than making the far less defensible argument of "I just don't like it"). It makes me more secure in who I believe myself to be. It's an ego boost.

And that's not such a bad thing. Perhaps I'm giving you the impression that I eschew anything fun or modern in favor of just slamming my students' noses in the book, but I don't. I'm all about mixed-media classes. The only difference is that I don't justify using a song as "being good for my aural learners." I justify it as being good for variety—as being a monotony hammer.

The fastest and most efficient way to learn a language point is purely through a first language textbook. If you're teaching comparatives and superlatives (i.e. more vs. most; -er vs. -est) the most stream-lined way to deliver the information will be in a tidy little table with color coding and a few pesky asterisks. After that, you do a few exercises, have a speaking, and bam: the students've got the idea.

Unless you're teaching highly focused robots, though, no one will want to learn that way. It's depressing and dull to work purely from textbooks and worksheets. It's monotonous—so much so that we need to mix things up just to keep the students engaged. So, for their benefit and—undeniably, our own—we've got monotony hammers.

Monotony hammers can be songs, interesting texts, memes you found online, jokes, drawing activities, a round of charades, whatever. Each group is gonna have a monotony hammer they have a preference for and from there we get the illusion of learning styles. It'd be a mistake to say that any and every time we use a song the students who are "aural" will learn more, though, because there are songs they inevitably won't like. It'd be a mistake to say that every game involving motion will benefit the "kinesthetic" learners either because sometimes competitions and movement are more of a distraction than an aid. See the difference?

You'll say I'm oversimplifying here. And, frankly, you're right. (Not about learning styles, though, I'm totally on point with those.) It's a disservice to refer to all learning materials as nothing more than "monotony hammers" because, in reality, a lot of them are actually what gives the language life. If all English were as cut-and-dry as a textbook then I wouldn't be writing this god-knows-how-many-pages-it's-gonna-be ramble. Whether it's a song or a magazine clipping, a lot of teaching materials actually give hope to students; they're a way of saying "hey, I know that this all seems like a death march of word lists and grammar rules, but don't forget that there's a world outside of it all. There are real live people who use this tangle of utterances to laugh, make fun of each other, call out their ex- for cheating on them with their best friend, and report on a cat that got saved from a telephone pole. That's encouraging.

Even so, you'll always have to get back to the book. Back to business. The rhythm of progress is monotony and it can only be broken up so much.

You can't plan for fun

Still, that doesn't guarantee that whatever monotony hammer you choose will actually *be* fun. More often than not, fun just *happens*.

My wife once had to teach a class about famous buildings—how tall they are, who built them, where they are, their architecture —just imagine trying to have a normal conversation about that, much less a class where everything already tends towards tedious and boring.

It was anything but that, though. The students really got into it. They already knew all the main information and had a bunch of trivia to offer—including something about an eagle that was trained to wash the windows of a skyscraper. Against all odds, it was a fun class.

Likewise, one of the funnest classes I ever gave was about family members and nationalities—neither of which we actually practiced. After blowing through all the material I had planned, we somehow wound up sitting around our little plastic table exchanging ghost stories. The two students I had were very young and had almost zero vocabulary, but they were determined to tell me every urban legend they could think of. "Ghost. See man. Man scared, but no run. He look back. There ghost. He look under bed and see picture of ghost. Man die." It was blast. With the help of a mini-whiteboard and some crude drawings, we could communicate just about anything.

We couldn't've anticipated this. Any good teacher will try to shape boring material from the book into something interesting, or even avoid it wholesale (there are some teachers who just chuck their books all together because they regard any book whatsoever as boring). But fun is a fickle fish; it tends to slip through even the best laid traps.

At one point my wife found a really nice Guess Who board game online. Typically we printed all our documents in black-and-white, but she figured this one was worth getting in color. She even wrote names for all the characters and asked for advice from three other teachers on how to teach her students "he/she's black" in the most PC way possible. She put a lot of time and thought into how she would use it because, honestly, it looked fun. We figured it would be a slam dunk.

Not so. One kid started pouting in the middle of class, refused to play, and the others were anything but enthusiastic. She got angry and forced them all to work out of the book.

Another example: have you ever heard of Hebocon? It's a Japanese battle robot contest where the competitors have zero technical skill. The robots they make are cobbled together from anything at hand. You can glue some remote-control cars to the bottom of a pizza box, name it "Amazing Quick Floor," and you'll make it to the semi-finals. If you win, you get a hodge-podge trophy which was "sincerely made by a third grader." I had a video about this madness and felt it was my *duty* to share something this awesome with other human beings.

But responses were very meh. The teens I taught just didn't get into it as much as I had hoped for. They weren't even excited to design their own crappy robot. I thought it was light years better than the canned dialogues from the book, but apparently I was wrong. I ask you: what healthy teenager can't get excited about a robot made of Lego pieces and a soup packet?

Other times the simplest activity can generate insane levels of fun. For the Japanese students I taught, everything was perfunctory: they arrived, mechanically told me "Iamfinehowareyou," sat down, opened their books, and started chugging grammar exercises. If we had an activity, whether it was writing their schedule for the week or playing charades, they did it with no zeal at all. The only time I ever got them excited was totally by accident. We were playing bingo and all they had to do was rattle off some sentences like "he likes bananas, he doesn't like cake" according to the pictures they had. I had bought some chocolates as prizes and the second they saw it, they flipped out. "HE'S GOT CHOCOLATE! HE'S GOT CHOCOLATE!" Never have I seen such rabid enthusiasm for cheap candy. It got to the point where I had to ban double bingos because they wouldn't stop screaming it.

Do you know the etymology of the word "happy?" If you've ever guessed that it and "happen" were related, then you're right on the money. In the same way "happen" and "happenstance" connote something out-of-the-ordinary which occurs randomly, the word happy was born out of this same principle. We don't get to make ourselves happy; we just set the conditions for it and, if we're lucky, we get that random burst of joy. Same case with fun—don't close yourself off to it, but don't count on it either.

Don't take it personally

I don't like collaborating. And no wonder: my wife points out that it's typical of teachers to be territorial ("this is *my* class and I teach it *my* way"). It's only natural that we suck at working in teams. Even so, every now and then we get stuck with an obligatory pair work activity in a conference or workshop and we just have to grit our teeth. (Mayhap it's karma for all the times we force our students to work in pairs in pursuit of "21st century skills").

One such time I had to plan a "Christmas quest" with my co-worker for a bunch of children. After preparing 80% of it myself, I decided to throw her a conciliatory bone. She would plan the scavenger hunt. The students would find various Christmas cards around the school following simple clues like "it's cold" to discover them in the fridge or "I'm hungry" to the vending machine. There were 12 cards and, to me at least, it seemed like the easiest thing in the world. She disagreed, though. She said it would take her an entire afternoon.

As I later realized, she was right. The day of the event, she gave me a bunch of haphazardly cut slips of paper saying things like "you might watch Rudolph again on the screen, screen, screen, though it once before you've seen, seen, seen."

No one understood anything. We had a kid who could barely manage the word "cat," much less the word "screen." So, we simplified. We rephrased everything on the fly and the kids wound up looking for and finding the items randomly.

I wish I could say that I stepped in to save the day after that, but everything I had planned went down in flames as well. We were both working from a misconception that our participants would have a minimal comprehension of English when some of them hadn't even moved past the alphabet yet. But what was done was done; we could only stick to the script.

From there, we did a logic puzzle I had painstakingly crafted which said things like "the chimney cannot be next to the elf who must be between the tree and bells but as far as possible from the mince-meat pies." Surprise: they didn't understand that either and ended up doodling all over the paper.

There was also a 20 question Kahoot which quizzed everyone on trivia like "how many reindeer pull Santa's sleigh?" "Which of these is a typical Christmas spice?" That one we only did half of because they eventually gave up the tedious task of reading in favor of random button mashing.

Then there was the finale: Christmas slime. I had found a recipe for peppermint scented, red & green Christmas slime on some mom-with-too-much-time-on-her-hands website. I had coordinated with the staff to get glitter, four bags of starch, four bottles of glue, and a bunch of cups for the occasion. In the end, they cheaped out on me and only got cinnamon rather than peppermint oil (plus there was no food coloring), but I figured it was good enough.

Funnily enough, at no point beforehand did it occur to me that I should try making the slime myself. Bad move: without measuring cups or spoons, we guesstimated everything and just poured more and more goop into our cups in the hope that somehow—*somehow*—we'd eventually reach a respectable level of consistency.

We never did. Amidst the encroaching fumes of cheap glue, the coordinator got frantic and rushed to open the window; she was cheesed off about the mess we'd made on the table and called the janitor to throw everything away. All through it, the kids were content to keep stabbing their cups of goo and pouring in the starch. Shame we couldn't let them.

I was beyond bummed out. After a nearly two-hour long parade of futility when my coordinator asked me "how'd it go?" the only response I could muster was "terrible. It was terrible." Expecting her to criticize me for the massive mess I'd made, I did her one better and criticized myself, admitting to not having planned thoroughly in regards to materials or the students.

I ranted uninterrupted about my own stupidity for a good minute, not letting her get a word in edgewise. It was a bitter confrontation (with myself—lame as that sounds) and the only good thing about it was its brevity.

The takeaway being? I'd screwed up, of course, but not in the way I angrily confessed to. I'd screwed up in that I took it all personally. Ironically, my colleague—who had almost no hand in the planning and execution of the event—dealt with it better than me. Despite having spent god knows how many hours writing sing-songy rhymes that no one would ever read, she checked in at the end, saw it was a complete disaster, and responded with a simple "oh. Okay."

Beyond that, there were the children—they were happy. They were happy to play along with our botched scavenger hunt. They were happy to mash brightly colored buttons even though they had no idea what answer they were giving. They were smiling and laughing all throughout the creation of the ill-fated Christmas slime and were unaffected by it all getting thrown away. That was the important thing to focus on.

But I was still caught up in the whole "I put a ton of time in this and it all went down the tubes" mentality. You can't survive with that mentality. There are few professions that require (*demand* even) unconditional love in the same way teaching does. There's a heavy emphasis on giving. You give yourself, your time, your enthusiasm (forced or otherwise) and even your money in pursuit of something that will likely be thrown into the rubbish bin without a second thought. At some point you need to distance yourself from the sting of rejection.

During my first year, I had a severe shortage of materials, especially for children's classes, and I sank a lot of time into making my own props for activities because the book just wasn't cutting it. For a section on telling time, for example, I stayed at the school late on a Sunday night making six or seven little clocks with moveable hands out of cardboard. They were pretty snazzy, lemme tell you, so snazzy that I didn't mind that the supermarket had closed by the time I finished, I didn't get to go shopping, and wound up having dinner at the 7-11. All told, I probably spent an hour making them, plus another half-hour of figuring out how I'd use them.

The following week, I distributed them to my awestruck students and proceeded to instruct them on how to play a game which no one understood. It was something like "run here, turn your hour hand to nine, run there, grab the token, move the hands back an hour, turn the minute hand, jump, hi-five your partner." It all made sense in my head, but in reality it was just me trudging around the room followed by a line of confused grade-schoolers. After 15 minutes I gave up and told the students to get out their books. It was gonna be yet another predictable class of filling out page after page of exercises. The clocks, for their part, got stashed in a bag and were never used again. An hour-and-a-half of work for 15 minutes of hectic confusion.

Even on occasions when I *did* get it right, the materials didn't amount to much. I remember one time I drew, colored and cut out a bunch of little clothes which I only used for three classes. Another time I made four detailed house diagrams complete with appliances and labels—those only lasted for one class. Then there were times when I never once used what I'd made: a PowerPoint, a worksheet, a drawing, a listening; my hard drive accumulated so many unused documents that I could've re-labeled the lesson plan folder as "graveyard of broken dreams."

Even so, I wouldn't have chosen *not* to make those materials. I know what I like. I've taught purely book-based classes, and I've taught classes which use the book as a springboard to something funner. Guess which one is more fulfilling.

There are times—and, being honest, they are *rare* times—when that extra activity makes a difference. I once gave 30-minute weekly classes to a woman who said she "just wanted to learn grammar." We had a book, but I only used it as a starting point or ignored it all together. One time we had a lesson on the difference between "could" and "was able to." The book gave nothing—*not even a flipping table*—to explain the difference, so I took it upon myself to prepare an example. I settled on drawing two pictures of a character named Joe fishing in a pond. The first one's a nostalgic memory from his childhood about how he "could" catch many fish. The second one's about his recent return to the pond as an adult; the shores are crowded with people, the water's choked with boats and pollution but, in spite of all that, he "was able to" catch many fish.

Have a look:

When Fred was young, (5-13) he went fishing every Saturday in a small lake close to his house. Since there were few fishermen at the lake, he _____ catch many fish.

1. How many times did Fred go fishing?

2. Was it difficult to catch many fish?

When he became a high school student, he was too busy to go fishing. But he had some free time last Saturday, so he went fishing again. The lake was very different. There were many fishermen and Fred had to stay for a long time, but

She ⟨ _____ ⟩ to catch many fish.

1. How many times did Fred go fishing?

2. Was it difficult to catch many fish?

I spent an hour or more drawing and inking those pictures, but her expression was more than worth it. The a-ha moment was so sudden and clear for her that she even gasped (Japanese people gasp a lot, but still). I was proud of myself in that

126

moment. I saved the original copies of those pictures and treasure them as one of my best mementoes of the year I spent in Japan. All that aside, though, that time investment, like so many others, came at a loss: an hour of work for a three to five-minute explanation.

Now, there are teachers who work exclusively from the book —lots of them. They carry the class on sheer personality and charm, working alongside everyone to finish exercises or give impromptu explanations. Sometimes they don't even check the book before the class to know what the topic will be. If they *do* prepare something beforehand, it'll just be a hastily printed page from the internet or a scan from a reference book. Not even that dampens their spirits.

I envy those people. If you can be one of them, more power to you. I can't, so the most I can advise you on is what I already know: it's an emotional commitment. Be prepared to give and give while getting very little in return. Above all, don't take it personally.

Time is a liquid, not a solid

If time were a physical object, what shape would it have? With calendars and schedules, we seem to have worked out that it's a square: it's a nice, tidy stack of blocks that composes the week and the year. With clocks, time is round: it's a continuously curling and spiraling sequence that we've conveniently pegged to the wall.

Out of these two, though, I'd argue that neither properly represents time.

Time moves differently in the teaching world than your contract will suggest. Ideally—mind you, in an *overestimated average way*—if you want to do your best without going overboard, half of your contact hours should be dedicated to lesson planning. If you've got 30 class hours a week, then 15 separate hours should be used for planning. If your class is three hours, then an hour-and-a-half should be dedicated to planning what you'll do. This is a broad generalization, but a useful one. It's also the extent to which we can confine time to blocks.

Why? Because time is leaky. Spend 45 minutes writing a sequence for a 90-minute class and you won't be done. You'll wait 5 minutes in line to use the photocopier at school, spend 3 minutes looking for paperclips, have to run back to make more photocopies when it's announced that you have a trial student, you'll have to frantically look for an administrator to replace the ink cartridge because it's spitting out stripes, then—with just 10 minutes to spare before class starts—you'll be hurriedly cutting out the cards from whatever game you've printed out, running from wall to wall rearranging chairs, writing instructions on the board, getting the CD player ready, and so on. Then —only then—will you be doing the hours you're paid for.

The residue of these contact hours isn't just restricted to planning either. Unless you're lucky enough to live within walking distance of your school, you'll have to factor in commuting times. That'll be 20 minutes on the train, 25 minutes walking, 25 minutes waiting for a bus—or any combination of those things. Unless you're lucky enough to work in a single class-room, you'll also have to factor in gathering up your books, your markers, your cables, your computer and whatever other materials you're using to run off to your next room, maybe even your next school which may be all the way across town.

Then there's the creative aspect of teaching. There are days when inspiration is a free-flowing resource; you look at the next chapter of your book and it hits you like a lightning bolt—I can use a song here, I can rearrange these two units, I can make a debate here, I can include an article I recently read, I can make a game out of this.

Then there are the dry periods where, for whatever reason, you sit there staring at the next two pages of the book unsure of what to do with them, feeling the preparation time available to you slowly draining away.

Time in class tends to splash and stain time in other places too. If you've got that one enigmatic group that just doesn't respond to games, just doesn't want to talk, just doesn't want to work from the book, then you'll be thinking about them elsewhere. It's not uncommon for me to have dreams in which I'm just repeating instructions or giving handouts in vain to a class of shadowy figures. I would never call them nightmares, though—just leftover time stains from the day.

Even the carefully arranged blocks of a school's schedule can melt and pool. In Mexico, punctuality was never a priority. Students made a point of arriving 15 minutes later than they were supposed to because, as they told me, it was a tradition. Traffic, weather, parents, chit-chat in the hallways, getting lunch, or any other reasons were given, but it all amounted to beginning and ending times that amorphously shifted with the week.

You'd say that's just a case of Mexican tardiness, but no. It was also the case with the Japanese students I had. I once had a student who almost never arrived on time, yet she still paid for an hour with me. Children sometimes would come 10 to 15 minutes late. Others rushed in at the last minute. Even now—with the strictest administrator I've ever had—I still get students who arrive from 15 minutes early to 15 minutes late. Other times the opposite happens: the class spills over into your break because the students haven't finished their exams or you've just got that one last point you need to make.

Even within the confines of the class, the more you grasp at time, the more it slithers through your hands. You'll calculate that a reading will take the students 15 minutes, but you won't factor in how long they'll need to calm down before they start reading—that's five minutes more. Next thing you know, you'll have to explain some vocabulary that you assumed they'd know—that's five minutes more. On the flipside, the debate you planned as a lead-in may get so intense that you refuse to cut it short because finally the students are using the language actively—that's ten minutes less. In short: things take however long they take.

Put a glass under the tap and the water'll fill the shape of the container. Pour it onto the floor and the water will spread out as far as it can. Likewise, give yourself an hour to plan a class and that's how long it'll take you. Give yourself 15 minutes and that's how long it'll take you. Granted, the latter class will be of dubious quality, but that's a point for another entry.

I used to plan all my lessons on the weekend and it took me an entire day to do everything because that's exactly how much time I gave myself. I once planned an hour-and-a-half long class in the backseat of a car while going to a clinic and it took me the entirety of the trip—about 2 hours—because that's how much time I had available. I once got hung up at the bank opening an account, had to rush back to the school, and planned two one-hour classes in 45 minutes because that's precisely how much time I had. I once arrived at school 15 minutes before class, realized I had forgotten all my materials at home, and slapped together a lesson for an hour-long class in that time alone.

I can already hear you giving me a "no duh." You, dear reader, have probably dealt with haphazard schedules already. You've pulled all-nighters, juggled friends and obligations. Maybe you've had a part-time job that was slotted willy-nilly into your schedule and you gritted your teeth through it. Whatever your experience was, you're no stranger to fitting work into odd places. You know how to be flexible because we all have to learn that lesson at some point.

Even so, I'm beating a dead horse here because there's a poignant exceptionalism to how teaching schedules work. The few times I've gone back home and picked up a part-time job after teaching have, weirdly, been more like vacations than working abroad has. The 8-hour workday is a beautiful invention of the modern world. It sets the perfect boundary between work and home; aside from maybe grousing about your boss to your family, there's a clear transition between when you work and when you rest.

That doesn't exist with teaching. Saying how long the job will take is virtually impossible. It seeps and spills where it will. You'll realize that once you start the job, but others won't. Friends, family, and—most importantly—employers will imagine all your classes as tidy little boxes that can be shelved and moved around Tetris-style all the while presuming that everything in between is totally free.

DISCIPLINE

You are the calm center of the hurricane

Discipline has never been my strength. I once fought a girl into doing her classwork by threatening to throw her shoe out the window. I'll readily admit that more than once I've snapped and ejected students from the classroom; I've dragged students still sitting in their desks into the hallway, I've tipped their desks forward and shoved them onto the floor, I've gotten frustrated and shoved a crumpled wad of paper into a kid's mouth, all because they either wouldn't listen or just wouldn't shut up. Not my finest moments, but there you have it.

For that reason, this isn't going to be a section about how to whip unruly classes into shape. I'm no drill sergeant; nor am I the smiling pacifist who negotiates a ceasefire through sheer goodwill. I've tried variations on both of those and always ended up somewhere in the middle.

When I started teaching three-hour classes with screaming, jumping children, I knew I'd have to toughen up. And that's exactly what I did. I marched onto the scene screaming commands. STAND UP. SIT DOWN. BOOKS OPEN. PAGE 13. BOOKS CLOSED. RUN. JUMP. WRITE. SILENCE. I cut kids off mid-sentence regardless of what they were saying. I adopted a twisted frown and forced myself not to smile. I yelled at kids for working too slowly—all in pursuit of cultivating a harder image.

That didn't work out so well, though. You have to speak loudly enough to be heard in the classroom, sure, but the consequence is that the students just speak over you; everyone's volume goes up, not just yours. By the time the next group came around, I had yelled myself hoarse. I would start coughing in the middle of a command and, to make matters worse, the students laughed at me for it.

So, I scaled back. With groups after that I did my best to talk through the noise, not over it. I stood at the front of the classroom, tapping my ear and repeating "guysguysguysguysguysguys" until I had everyone's attention. It had the benefit of saving my voice, but it was far from perfect. Getting everyone on the same page is near impossible, no matter how quickly or simply you speak. Someone always turns to chat with a friend, checks their phone, is daydreaming, or misinterprets what you say. That unleashes a cascade of errors where one kid turns to the wrong page, the others think he's got the right idea, then half the class is in chapter 4 while the others think they're supposed to be designing a menu for a vegan restaurant.

I bet you think I'm leading into an elegant solution here—that I'm gonna reveal some perfect middle ground between being the pushover and the hardcase. I wish. Truth be told, classroom management has more in common with disaster response services than teaching. Sometimes the helicopters scoop up the residents before the levee breaks, sometimes the hurricane just plows through everything and you're left to pick up the pieces.

I once gave a trial class to a 6-ish brother and sister. The class was an hour and ten minutes, far longer than their patience span, and the most I had to work with were some flashcards and a song. I was supposed to teach them the names of the characters from the book plus some functional phrases like "hello, my name is..." & "goodbye." Simple enough, I figured. I planned out a chain of reading, games, singing, maybe some coloring just to break the monotony, and otherwise I'd just recycle and improvise.

And it worked out pretty well. Up until the girl decided she was a caterpillar, that is.

I dunno what inspired it, but the girl just started flopping around on the floor—kinda like a seizure, just without the seizure part. I took my typical "that's very nice, dear, now let's get back to our game" approach, but she was unphased. She just kept wriggling around: under the desks, under the table, in and out of her chair, all while sporting a vacant smile. Her brother flipped out. He kept shouting "I'm telling grandma! I'm telling grandma!"

I tried coaxing her into playing with us. I tried playing only with her brother, ignoring her. I tried moving onto the next activity (the song, I think). I tried sitting down on the floor next to her, but nothing worked. Maybe there's a super special discipline technique I could've used here but, if so, I've never encountered it. The most I could do was wait it out.

"Wait it out" is about the best advice I can give on the discipline front. Of course there are always moments when the necessary action is obvious: if a kid's making sex noises in class, you tell him to stop; if a kid's smacking another one in the face with a ball, you take the ball away; if a teen decides to use the N word in every other sentence he writes, you make him do the whole exercise over again. Sometimes the havoc wreaked in a class is irreparable, though. In those moments, just remember—you are the calm center of the hurricane.

You might think it's just young learners I'm talking about, but sometimes a class of adults can be even worse. One such time I witnessed a conflict worthy of a soap opera. As it turned out, one of my students had been dating a teacher at the school (in secret, for obvious reasons). Her classmate caught wind of it and ratted her out. The news broke at about the same time as my class and the boyfriend was called into the administrator's office for questioning.

Meanwhile, his lover came to class all the same, but she was an emotional wreck. Try teaching ergative verbs to a woman who knows that her boyfriend is being grilled a few rooms over and that their relationship hangs in the balance. My spiel on how "the car drives into the garage" versus "I drove the car into the garage" illustrates both transivity and intransivity in one verb failed to console her in any way. All throughout she kept asking me for reassurance and I, being the schmuck I am, could only think to respond with the hackneyed "I'm sure it'll all be okay."

And it was most certainly not okay. If things weren't bad enough, about halfway through the class, the vindictive classmate popped her vindictive little head into the classroom and sneeringly announced "maybe you don't appreciate this, but everything I'm doing right now is for your own good. You'll understand that someday."

And out came the waterworks. The devastated girlfriend ran off to the bathroom, leaving the rest of us flabbergasted to awkwardly exchange glances and confirm "Yep. That just happened." Short of anything else to do, though, we got back to our ergative verbs.

You wield a certain authority as a teacher, sure, but that authority only goes so far. With children, things are more clear-cut: they don't know how to discipline themselves, so you become the pseudoparent. But with adults? Supposedly they discipline themselves, rendering you kinda powerless.

I've pondered *what* exactly I could've done in that situation many times, but I always come up short. Was I supposed to yell at the interloper? Accuse her of being a bad person? Or would that have just fanned the flames and gotten me mixed up in this whole mess? Should I have told my student to go home because she clearly couldn't focus? Should I have suspended the class and just turned it into an impromptu therapy session with the other students?

You'll have a lot of options on the table, but they all come with the potential to backfire. For that reason, I can only recommend that well known line from hostage negotiation movies: don't be a hero. That's someone else's job. Wait it out.

A baby's job is to cry

Not long ago I attended a teacher training class on teenagers. Fighting the cold, dark, flus, and traffic, all our teachers shuttled into the school's main branch. No one was sure what to expect, but everyone expected nothing. We weren't disappointed to see our expectations fulfilled.

The most I've ever picked up from trainings are quaint anecdotes. On this occasion it was a disappointingly brief story about train-surfing hooligans. Other than that, we introduced ourselves and swapped opinions. The consensus was pretty simple: "yep, teenagers are difficult. They don't want to learn, so you have to carrot-and-stick 'em." The enlightened lecturer then proceeded to affirm our comments: "indeed. Teenagers lack the cognitive development to intrinsically motivate themselves, therefore an educator must seek alternative means of motivating their language acquisition." We all nodded our heads thoughtfully, thanked the lecturer for his time, and finally got to eat the pizza they'd promised us. "Oh, yes," we told the 'big boss' (as the administrator called her), "it was nice. It was informative. It'd be great to have another one."

After failing to feel trained by the trainings I've been to, I've started to think that trainings don't exist for training, but something else. Solidarity is my best bet. After all, it's nice to whine with all your colleagues about an unresolvable problem while eating free snacks. It makes you feel less alone and less overwhelmed. At the end of the day, lesson aims will keep being vague in spite of all the inspirational quotes we read. Bad books will keep being bad in spite of how much we bang our heads together trying to make them better. Teenagers will be teenagers.

I know this first-hand because I'm guilty of having given my share of lousy presentations too. One was even on teenagers. I remember nothing from it other than throwing *the absolute worst* pages from my textbooks I could at my colleagues and asking them to figure out a lesson plan. When everyone looked just as miffed as I had upon first reading them, I cried out "ha!

You see? You see?"

What made those pages infuriating was the fact that they couldn't be simplified. The content was comparatives, but it wasn't just "Mt. Everest is the tallest mountain/Mt. Everest is taller than Mt. Fuji," no; instead the teacher was expected to review that with a jumble of intensifying adverbs like "quite, much, a little, much more" and "as...as" thrown in just for extra flavor.

It's a cinch to ask adults to learn these structures because A) they've probably already encountered it before and B) they're naturally curious and will probe the grammar to figure out how it works. They'll only do that because they've got the patience for it, though. For teenagers, grammar has to be more like a commando raid. Write an example sentence or two, highlight some words, dispense rules—bam. In and out in 5 minutes or less. If anyone gets left behind because they were goofing off, just point at the board. It's all there.

There's someone out there who will tell me everything to the contrary, someone who will tell me that teenagers are inquisitive and full of blossoming potential. It'll be a middle school math teacher, perhaps, who teaches their students to believe in themselves using macaroni and confetti to convey the intricacies of common denominators. And, swell. That person will probably get a movie made about them. They can have it. They can have my job while they're at it.

But, much as I hate to admit it, that person is right.

You've probably been scratching your head about the meaning of this section's title and how it connects to discipline. It sounds kinda zen, no? Perhaps it should come as no surprise then that I learned it from a pair of Japanese schoolteachers.

We used to meet once a week for a class that was half conversation and half translation. They had a book of single page reflections on life written by people from different industries (kinda like what I've written in this book, just much more reverent and inspiring). A lot of them were typical Japanese things about work, heritage and family that weren't memorable for me, but every once in a while we'd hit on a story which left me feeling refreshed as a human being. One such case was about a man who got annoyed by a crying baby on an airplane (I mean, who hasn't?). He complained to the flight attendant about it (I guess expecting them to chuck it out the window or something) and they, in true Japanese form, replied "it can't be helped. A baby's job is to cry."

This sounds like a cop-out. I know. It's the same justification people give for reckless and irresponsible behavior ("boys will be boys"). There comes a point, however, where our misfortunes have to be accepted as being out of our control. The earthquake knocks down your house enough times and you stop trying to build it out of wood—you use paper because at least paper doesn't crush you to death when it falls. Then, when you start building a city, you have no grand illusions about your skyscraper being untoppleable (yes, I just invented that word. Deal with it.)

On several occasions, I've witnessed teachers confront teenage classes for the first time. Their complaints are always related to behavior: they don't listen, they don't care. My bet is that a lot of workshops continue to exist precisely for these people. I was in the same position—still am, in many ways—and there'll be no end to the parade of other teachers that struggle to cope with teens.

Truth be told, it often seems that no one knows how to do it. Teens exist in a weird middle ground: they're both subnormal adults and irregularly overgrown children. That leaves an educator in the awkward position of figuring out which side to pay more attention to. And therein lies the error—forgetting that the baby's job is to cry, forgetting that the teen's job is to be an unhelpful jerk.

I have no grand illusions of becoming the subject of an inspirational movie about an educator who gives hope to the hope-less. That would take far too much work and I'd probably drop dead from exhaustion before I got anywhere. As one does in the elements, I aim to survive. I've learned to respect the forces of nature as inexorable. I work around/with them and I can only recommend that you do the same.

Be a wall to kick against

If you want an entertaining conversation with a teacher, ask them what has caused them the most grief in their career. Everyone's got at least one good story about a student or a class that ran them ragged.

In my wife's case, it was Super Safari—a group of temperamental toddlers. That course existed thanks to the patronage of parents with more money than sense. Everyone wants to give their kids an early start on learning English these days. The sensible ones understand that English classes should go hand-in-hand with real school. That socialization process is important; otherwise, you're chucking small human beings into an alien environment where they have no idea how to behave. But if you've got enough money, even reason can be paid off—hence, Super Safari.

There was a book for that class with creepy CGI pictures of animals. Each page illustrated a dialogue between the characters with an accompanying audio track. One dialogue, for example, was about the lion and the giraffe fighting over who would get to sit in a chair. In the picture, the chair lies broken on the floor, the lion and the giraffe look down with expressions of deep shame, the stern-faced professor zebra looms over them with his arms crossed. The lesson?—don't fight over chairs.

It sounds stupid, but that's a legitimate problem in classrooms. I once worked with another group of kids—not as little, but still pretty little—who quarreled about chairs every class. I had two types of them, one pink and one green and if the girls didn't get the pink chair, they'd throw a fit and derail the whole class. Eventually I had to swap my chairs with those of another classroom just to prevent further outbursts.

It's easy to scoff at the "values" section of a textbook. I roll my eyes every time I get a page about "the magic of sharing" or "why we shouldn't call each other stupid," but they're more valuable than their cheesy content suggests.

"Don't do that. It's dangerous." That warning alone can dissuade me from just about anything. Of course, I'll want to ask *why* something is dangerous, but the word itself—dangerous—already carries a significant semantic load with it. And, wouldn't you know it? That's a word that younger learners simply will not know.

I had a worksheet labeled "classroom hazards" at some point which focused precisely on that word. It had a picture of a computer room where students were supposed to circle all the "dangerous" things. I took one look at it and figured "oh, come on." There was a bucket of paint propped up on a half-open door, a bunch of loose electrical wires in a puddle, some kid was running with a cup full of scissors pointed sharp end up, and in the middle of it all was a guy playing basketball. I thought it'd be insultingly easy, but they ate it up.

After circling all the elements in the picture, the students took great pleasure in repeating their newly learned word. They pointed at everything with wide eyes, shouting "DANGEROUS! DANGEROUS!" This led to them walking around the classroom doing the same, pointing out half-hung curtains or a coughing air conditioner and shouting "DANGEROUS! DANGEROUS!"

I got a lot of mileage out of that word. Not just on that day, but for the rest of our time together. All I had to say was "don't do that. It's dangerous." and the students would desist.

It's easy to get angry at younger students, especially the really little ones because they tend to commit the most egregious violations of personal space or property. A lot of my students in Russia had this bad habit of wasting my markers. They'd just walk up, grab a marker, and start doodling all over the board with it—not even *pictures*, just lines and lines and lines. It was such an obvious waste and disrespect of my materials that I couldn't even respond to it. I just assumed that anyone with a shred of empathy would recognize it as wrong. My annoyance built up, though, and eventually I snapped and yelled at them. After that, they rarely if ever wasted my markers again.

I worried at first that yelling would be the only way to get results. With another group, though, I simply told the students —directly and firmly—not to do it. Surprisingly enough, they stopped.

I once worked with a guy who said younger learners are going through life like a swimmer through a swimming pool with no walls or floor. They'll shoot and thrash in any direction because, even if they want to swim, they ultimately need to know where the boundaries are. Give them a wall to kick against—a good, solid wall—and they'll even be grateful for it.

Let me end with another story about Super Safari.

One day my wife got her biggest problem child to finally sit down and do a worksheet. For some reason, though, his classmate decided to start playing cowboys and Indians. He made shooting gestures with his fingers, going "pew, pew, pew" and pretended to shoot problem child. Problem child got seriously disturbed by this and started crawling away, retreating under a chair with his worksheet, but the barrage continued. "Pew, pew, pew-pew-pew." It got so bad that problem child started to cry and my wife was forced to push the would-be-cowboy out into the hallway.

The cowboy kid had no idea what he'd done and my wife, not being able to speak Russian, couldn't explain the problem. She went outside, though, and with the help of cowboy kid's parent and the coordinator, eventually communicated the situation. Cowboy kid took it really well. He apologized not only to the staff, but also to the boy he harassed. After that, there was an unspoken armistice between them and no one got shot. Happy ending.

Don't knock the old ways

There was a private school my colleagues used to talk about in tones of gobsmacked dread. They told stories about having to teach in the hallway because the students were spilling out of the room. They said the students blatantly disregarded them, got into fights, bafflingly stole the erasers, and one teacher even told a story about how they had set the door on fire.

And as soon as I started there, I came to share their amazement as well.

The classrooms were poorly ventilated, concrete cubes where 20 to 25 of us were all packed in with an obstacle course of ramshackle desks. Only about a fifth of the students had the book. There was a whiteboard, but no markers or eraser. There was a projector, but to use it you had to precariously balance your computer on a desk in the middle of the room then snake a cable down from the ceiling. If it broke, you were pretty much SOL. I once asked the supposed tech guy to come and help me, but all he did was stand in the doorway and shrug. Apparently, he couldn't be bothered to fix the projector while a class was in session.

It was a thing to behold. They had sunk more money into advertising than the actual school. They had a catchy jingle and some giant letters spelling out the name of the school in the courtyard. The world outside was a different matter: the first time I opened the window, I did a double take at the incredible scene of desolation—crumbled houses riddled with weeds, a lopsided clothesline and a stray dog wandering lazily through it all. Another time, I glanced over to see what I thought was a streak of oil leaking down the wall only to realize it was a stream of black ants hauling a dead fly behind a wall outlet where, presumably, they lived.

I liked it. Better said, I liked it because it was atypical. It broke the mold for what I considered to be a normal classroom. It was challenging, incredibly frustrating sometimes, but ultimately rewarding.

At first, I approached it as much as I could in the "modern teaching philosophy" I'd been trained in. After all, that was why they hired us for, no? I tried using board games which encouraged conversation, but the students wound up fighting over who was jumping too many squares, not talking. I tried using the conversation questions in the book, but at most the intended discussion of "do you prefer watching local news?" or "do you watch sports on your phone or TV?" was "number 5?" "No." "Number 6?" "Yes." (And even that was assuming they spoke in English). I tried designing props for roleplays, but usually they just laughed at whatever I handed them and drew all over it.

What got me the best results with them was, unfortunately, the least inspired: worksheets. Lots and lots of worksheets. These kids would blatantly disregard a list of conversation questions but if you handed them a page of fill-in-the-blank exercises, they'd hop to it. I was sent to this school with the understanding that everyone would be learning natural, conversational English for real life use, but if anything helped them pass the end of course exams, then it definitely wasn't speaking activities, it was good old-fashioned copies.

Here I was—the herald of liberating, modern English instruction—being disregarded for primitive scraps of tree bark. It was dismaying, to say the least. All the more so when one day, while giving instructions, one of the chronically unfunny students said "¿¡y este por qué nos está hablando en Íngles si está en México!?" ("why's this dude speakin' to us in English when he's in Mexico!?") HAHAHAHAHAHA. Ha ha. Ha.

It was a telling comment. These students were accustomed to the old model of teaching: one where a teacher speaks their own language for the whole lesson, writes some grammar rules on the board, explains them, then everyone cracks open their grammar book to do such-and-such exercise. No speaking included.

You'll be told that this is dreadful. You'll be led to believe that we've moved past the anachronisms of the gatekeeping teacher model and that now total immersion is the way to go. The rationale is pretty obvious: by turning a student over to an English rich environment—with bona fide English speakers to boot —they'll be forced to learn the language even faster. Actually *using* the language is a massive improvement on just learning it from a book. Everything must be in English! We must speak even if it means prying the words out of the students' mouths like a dentist pries out a rotten tooth!

And OK. In general, it sounds swell. I've worked with plenty of students who are committed to this ideal, who speak exclusively in English even if it means being awkward and unnatural. When it works, it works well, but not everyone is cut out for that. The enlightened system only works for students who are enlightened enough to appreciate it. If that sounds unfairly harsh, it is; just keep in mind that you're not reading a teaching manual, you're reading a tirade with a highly liberal use of italics and contractions. Cut me some slack; while you're at it, cut the students some slack too. Not everyone is *willing* or even *wants* to learn English.

An example: imagine you were teaching adjectives of personality. How would you demonstrate them in a natural and meaningful context? I asked myself that and, channeling my CELTA instructors, decided to do it through well-known characters from games and movies.

I printed out pictures of Voldemort, Gollum, Harry, Darth Vader, Kylo Ren, Batman, Mario, Superman and a bunch of other obvious villains and heroes. I had the students sort them into "good guy" and "bad guy" columns on the board. I prodded them for details: "why's he a bad/good guy? What does he do/not do?" I introduced the vocab from the book. We read descriptions of other characters that included the target words—nasty, rude, patient, confident, and so on. I asked them to match the words with the pictures on the board. For each one, I grilled them for more details: "why's Gollum impatient?" "Because he can't wait for the ring. He needs it now." We played a game to practice the words. They described people in their own lives. Yada yada.

You'd've had to be sleeping to miss all of that. And yet? The next class, what do I hear? "Teacher, what's confident? Teacher, what's shy?" I anticipated some review would be necessary, sure, but it went beyond that.

How would you explain "dishonest" or "honest" in as few words as possible? Someone who lies? Someone who doesn't lie? Me too. I parroted that explanation a million times over to the very same students who asked me the very same question again. And again. One of them even shared in my consternation. When we were taking the test, he repeated my explanation verbatim accompanied by an "I. Say. Every. Class."

They *bombed* the unit test. And not bombed in an ironic reversal of meaning way by which it means "did well;" no, no, no, they did miserably. The highest score was, I think, a 53%.

Maybe I just picked the wrong characters? Maybe I shouldn't have said "lie" because they didn't know what it meant? Maybe the numerous times we played bingo, Kahoot, did crosswords, or worksheets were all inadequate for communicating the meaning of the words? Maybe.

Or maybe they simply didn't want to learn. Those kids were pros when it came to fill-in-the-blank exercises where you just have to change a given verb. They nailed those. As soon as you gave them a reading exercise or a word bank, though, they conveniently forgot everything. On that test there was a reading about Angelina Jolie and many of them wrote that she was "an American flying" who "is often in charity films such as *Tomb Raider*," "is very actress in her free time" and "likes does and owns a small plane." Simply put, they didn't want to think.

Sometimes I entertained the idea that I was being punished. I figured some kind of cosmic justice was being paid because, truth be told, I was just like these kids in middle school. I've worked my way up to a C2 in Spanish—the highest level there is —but it certainly wasn't any thanks to the three years of Spanish I took in public school. I was a brat. So was everyone around me. We spent the class shooting paper footballs at each other and talking about video games. Three years of Spanish and the only phrase I remembered was "no me gusta" because I used it for practically everything. The teacher even took me out of class once for a dressing down because I'd written "mi maestra es terrible" on a test.

But even if I could travel back in time to slap some sense into that brat I was, I wouldn't. It was my time to be terrible. I was happy scraping by with my studies, gorging myself on junk food, and playing terrible video games. I was a force of nature to be accepted.

By that same token, I gave up on the enlightened approach with my teens. I give them the class as they expect it: as a list of tasks to be completed. I make them write translations for vocabulary lists. They make ragtag flashcards which we practice mechanically at the beginning of each class. Everything else is comprised of worksheets; if they finish everything as scheduled, no homework. If they don't do the homework, they have to sit in "the dog box" and finish it the second they arrive. The most I do in the way of "fun" is the occasional write the word race.

It's old fashioned, but it continues to exist for a reason.

The elephant in the room

If there was an award for "Wikipedia article with the best title," "Execution by Elephant" would be a surefire winner. Open it and you'll immediately be greeted by a grainy illustration like something out of a morbid Victorian adventure novel. Turbaned onlookers recoil in horror, a kneeling man places his head chopping block style onto a stump, and an elephant slowly lowers its foot until—POP.

"Now, wait," you might ask, "why go to the trouble of raising, housing, and training an elephant just so he can slowly squash people's skulls open? Why not just kill the people normally and save time, money, and other lives which could also be squashed out of existence in the process?" A fair question—the morose answer is "because that's not nearly as fun;" the real answer, though, is "spectacle."

Execution by elephant is just one member of a ludicrously impractical family of execution methods; just think of drawing and quartering, the iron maiden, or the breaking wheel. For a more modern example, think of the electric chair. They're not efficient by any means, but they are extravagant; they lodge in the imagination of whoever witnesses them and instill a fearful reverence for the system that produces and maintains them.

You, however, will never have a trained elephant in the classroom to dissuade rule breakers. Too bad. Even so, the principle of spectacle still applies. You just have to be creative with it.

Remember that one private school I mentioned? The one with the giant letters in the courtyard that cost more than the classrooms themselves? I had a lot of discipline problems there. These ranged in levels of bad from students stealing the erasers to them sexually harassing each other.

I'm nonconfrontational at heart, so up till then I mostly dismissed everything with a "well, they're *choosing* not to learn, so it's hardly my fault." This I did in spite of no one managing to hear instructions or explanations because someone was always talking; in spite of people walking in and out the whole time on supposed "bathroom breaks;" in spite of fights; guys groping girls' legs; and one kid constantly playing with a Rubik's cube—even faced with all that, I clung to the belief that it was *on them* to behave, not on me to make them.

Besides, how would I even do that? Obviously reasoning and pleading were off the table—no one would listen to that. What's more, I had no authority in the school (I was a contractor, after all) it's not like I could threaten them with suspension or phone calls home. The one coordinator I could turn to was in and out all the time and, strict as she was, could only be relied on for an occasional finger-wagging.

I was in need of an elephant—several, in fact.

Excessive "bathroom breaks?"—hall pass: I bought a cheap plastic bus from a toy store, sloppily wrote HALL PASS all over it with a sharpie, then popped the wheels and stickers off it to make sure it was cumbersome and not fun in any way at all; I swore I'd replace it with the heaviest rock I could find if they ever lost it, but (sadly) they never did. As for the communication problems, I knew there were two problems: apathetic students and cellphones. The first was solved by breaking the class into a hierarchy. I made a bunch of dorky group leader badges which I doled out to trusted students every class; like generals, they were responsible for monitoring and transmitting my instructions to whomever was in their group for the day. As for cellphones: I just took them away. I got a big, crummy cardboard box and decorated the sides with sharpied happy faces and the slogan MAGIC CELLPHONE TREASURE BOX!

I won't lie and tell you that this solved all my problems, but it made everything a whole lot easier. My classes went from "out of control" to "refreshingly unpredictable." The students complied with my rules and even some of the worst ones showed progress. The only thing that made this possible, though, was the resources I put into it. Humor, for one, made the whole thing feel more like a game than a scolding. Intelligibility also made a big impact: it wasn't necessary to explain my methods or intentions with highfalutin language because it was all made explicit in symbols. The badges I gave conferred an obvious authority, they made the students into deputies of my will.

Could I have just put the cellphones into a normal box? Could I have made a normal bathroom pass or just counted who went in and out? Could I have made teams without the badges? Sure, but that misses the point: every rule needs something to back it up, an elephant in the background.

At the school where I worked in Russia, homework was an ongoing problem. A lot of students "forgot" their books at home, conveniently had no time between video games and soccer or simply didn't do it at all. In one class progress became virtually impossible because a handful of students would shirk their homework and come to class just to chat in Russian with each other. For all our appeals to the parents, this situation was never remedied.

So, I got an elephant. In the entrance to my classroom I had a long hallway which was cut off from the rest of the room. I tossed some desks in there and made anyone who hadn't finished the homework do it the second they walked in. I wanted to call it "homework hall," but the students—for lack of knowing the word "dog house"—rechristened it "the dog box." Whenever a classmate came in, the first question was always "homework?!" If the answer was no, they took great pleasure in chanting "dog box! Dog box! Dog box!"

I repeated it for another class which, in truth, I didn't have many problems with. Even so, one too many classes without homework and I told them "look. You don't do the homework—dog box." Then I kicked one of the desks into the hallway where the table clattered off to create a dramatic illustration of my point.

They ate it up. Chastising them for being lazy or getting angry would've been far less effective. For one, it would've lasted only one class (unless I wanted to waste energy on the same thing every time they forgot their homework); for another, it would've turned them against me. The dog box had the opposite effect: it could be enjoyed and appreciated as a joke, even if they were the butt of it. It was more spectacle than punishment.

While I'm on this topic, I'd like to bring up a bit of apocrypha. You know that decade when boomboxes were all the rage and people lugged them around on their shoulders, blasting music for all the world to hear? Legend has it that there was a high school teacher who had a personal vendetta against these things. "If you ever bring a boombox into my classroom, I'll hurl it straight out the window," he threatened, to which the students presumably laughed, thinking it was all hyperbole.

But he intended to make good on his threat. He scrounged through a few dumpsters until he found a boombox someone had thrown out. He cleaned it up, planted it in the classroom before anyone had arrived, then left. That day he was the last one to enter the classroom. After walking in, he spotted the boombox, put on a big show of being angry, and then—just as promised—chucked the thing out the window. It flew a few stories down then burst into a million little bits on the pavement below. From that point on, no one dared to bring a boombox into his room.

I can't source that story. I know I read it online somewhere, but Google searches haven't turned anything up. It may well be purely fictitious, but it's not so much the story as the moral of it that matters. When you've got a problem, you need a rule; when you've got a rule, you need something to back it up. In an environment where your powers are limited to red pens and phone calls home, that's hard to do. That's why everyone ought to have an elephant in the room.

Simplify, simplify, simplify

Did you know the early Mongols were all illiterate? I mean, it's kind of obvious: with all the hunting, constructing felt tents, riding horses, falconry, and just surviving in the harsh climate of the Asian steppe, there's not much room for books. Still, though, it begs the question: how did a bunch of unlettered bandits pull together an empire, much less the transcontinental military campaign to form one? To use Jack Weatherford's analogy, it would be like a slave from the early Americas cobbling together an army to conquer all the land from New York to Brazil. How on earth do you do that?

Well, to cite Weatherford again, through song. Across regiments of tens of thousands of troops, the great khan's battle orders were set to a well-known melody so that—if pieces were lost or misinterpreted while playing telephone between generals—the final message would always be clear as having or lacking all its components. No verse, no couplet, no rhythmic foot could be omitted.

Whaaaaaaaaaaaaaa-?

Yes, I know. I was highly skeptical too (so much so that I'm putting Weatherford's name here just so I won't be accused of making harebrained claims about ancient history). But the more I thought about it, the more it made sense to me.

If there's anything that can really burrow its way into your memory, it's a melody. Much to my shame, I can still recall every single word of the Pokemon theme song to this day. I swear, on my death bed my descendants will be leaning in to hear my final words:

"I want...I want..."

"Yes, father?!"

"—to be the very best."

And then I'll die. If they don't Google it, they might just think I've said something profound. Not to say the Pokemon theme song isn't *already* deeply profound, but it could be even more so. If I could encapsulate all my important life lessons into the melody of that song, I'd be set. I'd never forget to turn off the hot water heater after a shower, wash the dishes, or wind up stranded at the train station because of the lunchtime break.

Take the "Head, Shoulders, Knees and Toes" song. Learn it once and you've learned it for life; best of all, just like a serial killer's freezer, it comes loaded with body parts. You would be stupid *not* to use this song with a group. If you incorporate the dance alongside the lyrics, you'll've literally pointed out every part of the body therein referenced without any explanation necessary.

You know "Baby Shark?" If not, I envy you; it's an annoyingly catchy song about a family of sharks that was made by a team of Koreans dressed up as cotton candy colored animals. In a word: mesmerizing. Never have I encountered a child who was unimpressed by it. The bright colors, animations, and super-simple lyrics make it understandable for everyone. And, once again, it transmits vocabulary for family members incredibly well.

Be it music, mnemonics, dances, gestures, weird noises, etc., anything simple but memorable has an immense ability to transmit information. You, as the teacher and a native English speaker, will go into the job brimming with technical terms like auxiliary verb or subordinating conjunction and, if you've done your homework, you'll know exactly what they mean. It's tempting to just leave it at that, to just tell your students "this is the present perfect, use the preterite here, where's the demonstrative pronoun?" but doing so will only work for the most lettered of your students (and good luck with that if it's a group of children).

There's one particularly pesky verb which will illustrate this well for you. If I had my way, I'd remove it entirely from English because it's empty. "What it do?"—nothing, really. It no does nothing because it no has any individual meaning. People would understand you perfectly if you no used it, but for some reason we no do that.

It's impossible to sell students on the use of "does/doesn't/ don't/did/didn't" because no other European language uses it. If you want to say something negative in the past, "I ate" usually becomes "I no ate." If you want to ask a question, you say "you ate?" and the rising intonation tells our brain that we're asking a question—no helper verb needed.

This is what we got stuck with, though. As teachers, we just have to teach it; and, believe me, it's no easy feat. I've dabbled with countless tables to simplify the "do/does/is/am/are" conundrum into something manageable, but an elegant solution eludes me. For all my fussing, I still wind up with sentences like "do you a doctor?" or "he don't likes ice cream" or "you does is Mary?" Throw in the word reversal of "she is a doctor/is she a doctor?" and you've got a recipe for disaster.

So. In lieu of a magic bullet, I've resorted to hand gestures and phrases. For example:

- "She is Mary?" → make a swapping gesture with your hands
- "He don't know" → draw an "s" with your finger
- "She doesn't swims" → repeat the refrain "no double 's'"
- "They didn't walked to school" → repeat the refrain "no double 'd'"
- "He don't a doctor" → repeat the refrain "no verb"

I'm not the first one to do this and I won't be the last. Doubtlessly there are people out there with far more sophisticated methods than what I'm using, but I've yet to meet them. The fact that these methods exist in the first place testifies to a significant fact: you can communicate meaningful information without specific words.

Well, duh.

I know, but bear with me. In this field, it pays to remember the adage "the more you talk, the less you say."

I came into my first job fresh out of college with my brain full of bombastic words like "hegemony" and "ostensibly;" I pronounced "comparably" with three syllables rather than four; I prided myself on having a truly "copious verbiage." What's more, I had engaged in so many high-brow Socratic seminars that pretty much every discussion I had became an exchange of verbal essays where you could practically see the semicolons and dashes between breaths.

On some level I stupidly assumed I could continue in this vein when talking to my students. On Monday mornings, I worked with a group of lovely old ladies who only wanted to read and discuss news articles. Per their request, every weekend I scoured the internet for interesting headlines, copied and pasted the articles into word documents, and edited out all the difficult or superfluous words until they occupied only a page (harder than it sounds, believe me).

Whereas a normal, competent teacher would've started out by establishing the context of the article teaching new vocabulary, I just slapped that sucker down on the table and got them reading. After reading, the same teacher would've patiently waited for his students to initiate conversation themselves, even provided some comprehension questions. Not me—the second those women finished, I pounced. "So, in your opinion, did Al-Qaeda behead these people and bury them in a mass grave because they were involved in counter-terrorism measures or merely to send a message to civilians about who's boss?" (That question isn't verbatim, but I'm sorry to say I did once give them a beheading story).

Things continued like this for about two months. I got better articles, fortunately, but the atmosphere was still really tense. So tense, in fact, that I dreaded the class a little more every time. I talked to fill that awkward vacuum of silence, but the more I talked the tenser things got. The spiral continued downwards and each week I got more and more frantic. I was convinced that they would complain to my boss and I'd be packing my bags to return home in no time.

I burned myself out. Exhausted, I gave them the article, stared in defeat at the table, and waited for them to finish. There was the usual silence. I continued staring at the table. The silence dragged on.

"This is very interesting," one of them finally said. The other students concurred. Then a conversation started—one I was largely absent from. It was the best class I'd had so far, and all thanks to one simple fact: I'd shut up.

I learned a lot from those women about how to manage a conversation. The key, as with everything in teaching it seems, was to simplify. This translated even to the most basic things. In the beginning, if one of the students told me "I really liked this story," I'd respond with a long-winded "me too. I think it's a great story about challenging yourself to be the best you can be" and no one would know what to say next. They'd be overwhelmed by the mass of verbal garbage I'd just chucked at them. Saying just "me too" was a big improvement, but even better than that was saying nothing at all, just saying "mhm." No matter what language you speak, that's a universally understood response.

Even coordinating turns between students benefited from simplification. I used to say "that's very interesting, Keiko, I especially like your point on the difficulties of implementing crop rotation strategies in rural communities; what do you think, Yoko?" But that was better said as "very interesting, Keiko; what do you think, Yoko?" or, even better, just going "ah. I see," and gesturing to the next person I wanted to talk.

Interestingly, this principle applies to the teacher as a person as well. There are two types of "best" teachers I've had throughout my life: those that were interesting as people, and those that helped me learn in an effective way. Funnily, I can remember the names of the interesting ones, but I can't tell you what they actually *taught* me. Vice versa with the effective ones: the classes where I felt I was making the most progress were taught by… someone?

Scribner says that a teacher has to be authentic. If you're not yourself in the classroom, it'll only cause you discomfort and the students will catch on pretty quick. Even so, you're not paid to be yourself. It's valuable to add a personal touch to a class, but you're not the main event; you're a sideshow; not even that —you're the lights guy, you're the audio mixer, you're the dude selling tickets at the entrance, you're the janitor and the hired security; you make the concert possible, but you aren't the concert yourself. Just step back and let the people enjoy the show.

It's all about that one shot

If you haven't figured it out already, I'm a huge dweeb. For precisely that reason, I'm about to make a Star Wars analogy. Consider yourself forewarned.

You know how two of the original movies revolve around destroying the death star as the ultimate goal? It's pretty much the same story except that the first one is this sleek, efficient death machine which offers up nothing but a little hole for its destruction. Meanwhile, the second one was so exposed that you could drive a truck through it. It's no wonder that the third movie gets panned for not having the same gravitas as the first; whereas one seemed like an impossible battle against the-evil-to-end-all-evils, the third was just a romp on an alien moon with a bunch of teddy bears.

Anyway, whether it's "restoring peace to the galaxy" or just getting your job done in the classroom, we've all got a potentially fatal death star to destroy. Ours just so happens to come in the form of students.

Imagine you're teaching the present perfect for the first time (e.g. I have been to London, she has eaten octopus, we have ridden a camel, etc.). If you've got a class full of adults, they'll be like the second death star—full of open spots to fire your... "grammar"... blaster... I guess. Eh, you get the idea.

Right from the get-go, they'll be analyzing the dialogue in the textbook and providing their own answers. Fill-in-the-blank grammar boxes were made for these kinds of people because they'll zoom in on any new constructions they find and immediately ask questions. From those questions, you get your shot to give the explanation of a lifetime. Nail it and the death star explodes, everyone oohs and ahs and the credits roll.

But chances are you won't nail it the first time. You'll get distracted by other questions. You won't have a singular answer to such a multifaceted topic. (No one does for present perfect, at least). And that's okay. The questions'll keep rolling in even if you flub the first few.

Not so with younger students. For them, you've got just one shot. Assuming you've navigated the turret riddled canals in your tiny ship, popped on your cross-hairs helmet and dodged those pesky fighters zooming in and out, there'll be that one moment where you get your shot.

In my first class with real-live, apathetic, grumbly teenagers, I missed that shot all the time. At first I just relied on the grammar boxes in our textbook. They'd read the text, copy-and-paste phrases from it, then blithely say "I don't understand" when the exercises came up. "So. They don't like the grammar boxes," I concluded. "No biggie, we'll do it all on the whiteboard."

From there I tried mapping out the sentences on the board with different colors. I called up students to fill in blanks, had them repeat phrases, asked for more examples. The whole thing felt very thorough, especially since it took a good 20 minutes. And then? "I don't understand," they told me yet again.

"But the rules are right there on the board." They squinted feebly at the jungle of arrows and dotted lines on the board, dazzled by it, then looked back to me again. "I don't understand."

Every freaking time.

And it's not like they couldn't understand. They just didn't want to.

So, I simplified. I remember with that particular group I once had to teach the difference between "for" and "since" (for: ages, months, days, weeks...; since: last week, a month ago, yesterday...). At first, I did what the book did: I drew timelines. I represented for as a duration which could be recognized as having a beginning and end. "Since" was a duration with clear start but no end. It was all beautifully rendered on the board with sweeping arcs and dipping lines. And what'd they have to say about that?—the same, infuriating "I don't understand."

It wasn't just a matter of apathy either. While I was fiddling around with my artistic lines, they were chatting and sharing candy in the background. Every time I shushed them, I'd lose my train of thought and lose whatever meager attention I'd wrangled from them. Even so, I was content to plow forward. I was like that one fatso out of *A New Hope* who just repeats "stay on target" until he nosedives into the Death Star.

You know what finally did it? Something so stupidly simple even they couldn't pretend to not understand it: Since/For. If you can't make it plural (i.e. add an S to the end), use since. For everything else, use for. There were exceptions to the rule, of course, but in general it encapsulated the whole idea. It was a rule no bigger than a womp rat delivered at that key moment when all eyes were on me. Boom. Roll credits. Pull out your workbook.

ON LEARNING THE LOCAL LANGUAGE

It's all up to you

Learning the word for "take-away" in Japanese was one of those magical aha moments. I was on vacation somewhere and I stopped at a café for lunch. I was placing my order at the counter when the cashier asked me "here-----or------hold-return?" A lot of the question was white noise to me, but the context plus the self-explanatory nature of that compound made it all click in an instant. Hold-return! It was so obviously constructed! So much so that I was inspired (complete with hand gestures) to say it out loud. "Ah! hold! Return! Of course!"

The guy behind the counter wasn't nearly as excited. He forced out a confused smile then, pausing, gave me this look like "yeah, that's great, bud. Now take your bagel and go. You're holding up the line."

Needless to say, we didn't become conversation partners.

Being in the language rich environment of a foreign country, your brain almost forces you to recognize patterns like this. Even if you're just visiting for a week, chances are you'll walk away knowing how to say "please, thank you, money, restaurant, exit, entrance" and any other practical word that pops up throughout your journey. It's beguiling. It lures you into thinking "well, if I've learned all this just during a vacation, after a year I'll be speaking the language just like a native!"

Not so.

It's an attractive and seemingly intuitive thought that, by pure osmosis, you'll pick up a language. After all, children do it. Why shouldn't an adult be able to do the same?

For starters, the conditions are different. Think about the advantages a child has versus an adult:

- they're a fly on the wall—they get to eavesdrop on every type of conversation imaginable and thereby pick up bits and pieces of each one by virtue of repetition (as an adult, you're only privy to conversation typical for the company of adults, you can't well sit in on a conversation between children at a playground without someone calling the cops);

- they're forgiven as adorable when they make mistakes like "you're the bestest dad in the world" or "I saw a wabbit," and through gentle, loving correction, they eventually learn what's right (say that as an adult and you're just written off as creepy or stupid—no corrections included);
- they're subject to a barrage of media designed specifically for children which simplifies the language down to its most basic components—what's more, they have the time to indulge themselves in it (for an adult, this would just be irritating, boring, and impractical);
- they're free from the entanglements of specialization: instead of having to learn specific vocabulary for their career as a lawyer, their conversation with the plumber, or paying their bills, they get to pick and choose what words to incorporate into their lexicon, be it "plesiosaurus" or "supersonic death ray."

Above all, they just have more time. Think about how long it took *you* to learn *your* first language. By the age of ten you could get by in almost every interaction. Not like you could bluff your way though a job interview at NASA, mind you, but you could negotiate any everyday conversation.

By college it was the same thing, just more intensive. Even now, as an adult, you're *still* building that lexicon with useful terms and colloquialisms. You're learning to talk about politics. You're gathering functional language for defusing arguments or winning them. You're coming to grips with whatever new technology has been loosed on the world.

Now do that all again, just in a second language and without the societal framework to support your development.

But wait! What about the "children's brains are different from adults' brains" argument!? Don't children have some sort of vague plasticity and absorbency to their brain which allows them to magically learn another language? As an adult, maybe it's not just the environment which encourages and enables your language acquisition! Maybe my brain just isn't able to learn!

I don't buy it. I'm no psychologist, but the many people I've heard make this argument weren't either. And while it may be true that a child's brain is more geared to learn a new language, that doesn't mean an adult brain is *incapable* of learning. It's a cop-out. It's an easy way to dodge a daunting responsibility—that it's all up to you.

When I went to Japan, I expected to pick up the language within a year. Not fluently—I wasn't that stupid—but I *was* stupid enough to believe that I could learn it with the same efficiency I'd learned Spanish. I'd been hacking away at that one for my whole college experience—four years—and I knew my grammar and vocab by heart. I'd made over 10,000 flashcards which I practiced religiously and considered myself a pro. Clearly, I thought, I had a knack for language and I'd be able to apply it with even more success the second time around.

So, I threw myself into it. Fast forward a year, a thousand-some flashcards, one to two hours of practice a day, four textbooks, three teachers, several animes, and a few kids' books. Where did I end up? Pretty much nowhere—barely with the proficiency necessary to ask "Can you tell me which train goes to Hiroshima?"

I blew it. I mean, obviously I'd set myself an unrealistic goal, but all the same it felt like I'd screwed everything up. Maybe on some level I was aware of how preposterous my goal was, but I didn't want to accept it. I preferred to buy into the myths about how living abroad would magically flip some latent language switch in my brain and, not surprisingly, I'd come up short.

Truth is, I didn't have a chance. If I'd been living in a zero English environment and every waking hour had been dedicated to studying then maybe—*maybe*—I could've breached the B1 to B2 level. As things stood, I only could've managed a modest A2.

But don't just take my word for it, look at what the experts have to say:

Category I language: 95 or higher (French, Italian, Portuguese, and Spanish)

Category II language: 100 or higher (German, Indonesian)

Category III language: 105 or higher (Hebrew, Hindi, Persian Farsi, Dari, Punjabi, Russian, Serbian/Croatian, Tagalog, Thai, Turkish, Uzbek, and Urdu)

Category IV language: 110 or higher (Modern Standard Arabic, Iraqi Arabic, Chinese, Japanese, Korean, Levantine Arabic and Pashto)

Through years of making troops into linguists, the Defense Language Institute (DLI) has developed this ranking system. If you're a native English speaker, you'll have the easiest time learning Category 1 languages; from there on, your job just gets harder and harder.

(And, wouldn't you know it? There's Japanese—smack dab at the top of the chart).

In the DLI, the troops have such intensive training that they can turn out effective speakers of these languages within 36 weeks (1&2), 48 weeks, and 64 weeks, respectively. Let that be a lesson to you: if the US armed forces—with all of their firepower and research—can achieve those results, then how can you—as a meager individual—hope to do better?

It's a steep hill and climbing it (or even starting it) is all up to you.

I once worked with a guy who had lived in Japan for 7 years. Let's call him Fido since when I gave my students his real name, they asked "isn't that a dog's name?"

Anyway, Fido had lived in Japan for 7 years. This is the part where I'm supposed to tell you "and he spoke perfect Japanese," but the truth is he didn't. While I was there struggling with kanji stroke order and transivity pairs, this dude was content knowing nothing more than "where're the vending machines?"

Nothing odd for someone working in a country where everyone knows a smattering of English, I suppose, but he had a Japanese wife. And kids. Two kids, at that. I can't say for how long (or if) he lived with them, but he was involved in their lives—albeit at a distance. He took them out on the weekends, he spoke of them in glowing terms.

This was the mind-boggling part for me: if Fido was interested in being a supportive father then shouldn't *literally learning to communicate* have been priority number one for him? Didn't he realize his kids would grow up barely able to speak with their father unless he took action? Didn't he value the country which gave him a place to work and live?

Outside of work and his kids, his other main use of time was going to clubs where he'd pick up chicks. If nothing else, you'd think knowing what they said about him when they gossiped would at least be worth his time. Maybe he could've even polished his pick-up act this way.

As for the country he lived in, he certainly didn't like the part of it he inhabited. He openly complained—in class to his students, nonetheless—about how boring their hometown was because there were no nightclubs; he said its only advantage was being a few towns away from a US airbase where he could buy Uncle Ben's rice. It's not like he didn't have time for studying either; he spent that on video games instead.

My Japanese teacher was similarly baffled. He taught classes for foreigners at the local university where, to Fido's credit, he had enrolled. The confusion wasn't at that, though (nor was it because of his 7 years of Japanese-less-ness); my teacher was baffled because Fido only showed up for a few classes then—POOF—he was never seen again.

The point I'm making here isn't one about being a good father or a responsible teacher (nor is it a cheap shot at Uncle Ben's rice —which is awesome, by the way). No, the moral of this story is what I've said twice already—it's up to you. I legitimately believe that language is the most meaningful medium of connection we as humans have with each other, but just being human doesn't entitle you to it.

Maybe my colleague realized that and—faced with the tedium of learning a language all over again—simply threw in the towel. Maybe he sold himself on the "only children can learn a foreign language" line. Or maybe he just felt his "job" was already done because he was paying alimony and seeing his kids on the weekends. He was working, he was earning money— what more should life ask of us?

Halfway through our Russia contract, my wife and I spent our Christmas holidays in Mexico. On the flight back, I was plugging away at my Russian grammar sheets when the guy sitting next to us decided to strike up a conversation. "I used to be just like you," he said, almost wistfully.

He had studied Russian in earnest for two years and then, just like that, he let it slide. He was still working for a car company in Russia, but he had run out of steam. "I've already learned French," he rationalized, having just ordered a drink from the French flight attendant with flawless pronunciation, "I've done my part."

And if that's how he felt, that's how it would be. No one—not the guy at the café who gives you your bagel, not your wife and kids, not the people at your company—is gonna make you learn. It's all up to you.

Which raises the question: why do it then?

Career-wise, an English teacher who speaks the local language is an attractive option for a school, sure—even more so for the students who have their own living dictionary to consult. But schools don't mandate that simply because they *can't*. There's *no way* they could fill their quota for each year's turnover.

Maybe it's good to practice what you preach? It smacks of hypocrisy to have a teacher who, on one hand, urges his students to study more and then, on the other hand, doesn't even try to learn the language of the country he lives in. It's not like your job depends on it, though. You're not a diplomat or an interpreter.

Out of respect for the country you're living in? It sounds nice in concept and maybe you'll get some applause or nice bonding moments with students because of it, but that's about it. More concretely, you could argue it's for connecting with the "locals." One guy I worked with, for example, went out with Russian girls he met on Tinder and enjoyed chatting them up in Russian, but even he admitted that English was their go-to-option for intimacy. As he pointed out, you're not yourself in a foreign language. "The Russian me is boring."

It's a difficult choice to justify. I've grappled with Japanese for about four years now and the most I've gotten out of it is some squiggly calligraphy (which makes for nice decoration, at least) and an N3 on the Japanese Proficiency Test. I'm not gonna use Japanese for my job, though, and I don't have any Japanese friends, so... at best... what? It's a hobby. It's a curiosity. It fulfills me, but not much else.

I decided to run the whole gamut again with Russian, but these days I find myself asking why? For what? My wife started out studying with me but eventually opted out. Russian gave her zero satisfaction, so she went back to studying French. She learns song lyrics, talks to people through Italki, and in general seems to just have fun with it. Meanwhile, the most I can show for my efforts is a growing stack of declension tables. Occasionally I can tell strange people at the train station that I don't want to buy knock-off Lacoste shoes (but, honestly, one can already do that with gestures).

I like it and all; I like cracking open a language and seeing how it works, but I'm well aware that it's not for everyone.

I can say I study—and teach abroad, to a large extent—out of pure linguistic tourism. I'm building up a cabinet of linguistic curiosities which I'll someday use for... a book, maybe? A master's? I'm still not sure. What I *am* sure of, though, are the techniques I've developed for catching and classifying my linguistic specimens. For what it's worth, here they are.

Meaningful repetition

That's it.

Two words.

You can dig through a million different bloggers and polyglots online who'll claim to have found a secret method for learning languages, but theirs will always fall into those two words: meaningful repetition.

I'm partly plagiarizing Stephen Krashen's theory of comprehensible input here (see: https://www.youtube.com/watch?v=fnUc_W3xE1w&t=32s), but I'm rephrasing it a bit for my own purposes.

Look: the first song I learned to sing in Japanese was "If You're Happy and You Know it, Clap your Hands" (the second song I learned was "I'm So Sad I Can't Go On," which really shows how downhill my life went from there, but anyway...). There's a line in the lyric which uses the word "taido." I had no idea what the word "taido" meant at the time, but I dutifully sang it all the same. That lodged it in my memory.

Not long after, I learned that "taido" meant attitude. It was from another source, but I made the connection right away. In my brain, the information was filed away as

ATTITUDE = THAT ONE WORD FROM THE CLAPPY HANDS SONG.

If I ever forgot the word, I'd just sing the song again (yes: with the hand clapping because I'm an idiot like that) and, voila, there was "taido." It worked the same when I learned the kanji for taido: I filed it away as

THESE SQUIGGLY LINES = ATTITUDE = CLAPPY HANDS SONG.

But the kanji is a bit of a mess:

態度

Pretty and all, but a pain if you don't recognize the individual elements. Luckily, I made some connections for that too:

能 = ABILITY + HEART (心) = = ATTITUDE = CLAPPY HANDS

Luckily the second kanji clicked in my brain as just

度 = TIME(S)

but I don't usually get that lucky. Remembering the kanji, and/or words by extension, is like trying to recount a hazy dream over breakfast: "there was a horse... I think. It was crossing a river next to a mountain which was actually two mountains stacked on top of each other. Then there was a farmer above a rice field, but one of his legs was longer than the other for some reason..."

There's a whole book dedicated to that. Heisig's *Remembering the Kanji* is a walk through an art gallery full of moons and shell-fish with a tour guide who tells you things like "the eye watches a mouth from which legs are protruding," "a hook draws out the tongue of a riot."

It's a trip. If it wasn't, then you wouldn't remember it all so well. Kanji are a jumble of primitive drawings derived from turtle shell etchings which nowadays have been randomly jumbled into meanings. The oft spouted "baka," for example, is a combination of the glyphs for horse and deer. Little wonder: only an idiot would mix up those two animals. Next you'll be mixing up mountains, trees, and rivers and claiming they represent totally unrelated words.

Wait a second...

Anyway, you see those elements repeated all the time. Same case with any aspect of language. We, as humans, suck at remembering everything, but we're awesome at recognizing patterns. To take advantage of that, languages have a built-in redundancy: redundancy of grammatical forms, word constructions, intonation patterns, what-have-you. Exploit that and you'll be well on your way to communicating.

You—the learner of X language—just need to turn redundancy to your advantage. To that end, I offer the following suggestions:

- **Textbooks:** pirate them. Seriously—it's nice to get a physical copy of a beginner textbook, but you'll blow through it pretty quickly, most will run you a good $20-30 each (if you're lucky), and sometimes the best materials won't even be available in print. Plus, it behooves you to juggle your materials as most will be antiquated or geared towards specific audiences like college students or businessmen (I've suffered through far too many dialogues about Japanese office lackies discussing why the copy machine is broken).
- **Flashcards:** haters of flashcards will dismiss them as robotic and boring. Both charges are true. Even so, they're a surefire tool for driving things into your skull. I ran through my thousands of Spanish flashcards so many times in college that now I couldn't forget them if I wanted to. If you don't mind them being robotic, download an app like Anki; if you want them to have more life, write them out by hand (some say that this improves retention rates anyway). Boring though they may be, they replicate a very real learning process: your brain picks up words that it sees on a regular basis; you may not be able to spend a whole lifetime learning words in situ, but you can just as well recreate the frequency aspect at home.
- **Word Frequency Lists:** to feed your flashcards. Most online dictionaries will have these. Use them. Learn the simplest synonyms first and the rest will follow.

Don't know the word for "manufacture?" Use "make" instead. Don't know the word for "steal?" Use "take." These words provide a useful fallback when your fancy words fail you. Plus, they usually provide the rudiments of more complex compounds. In Russian, for example, you learn the word for "do," snap a prefix on it and you've got the word for "finish" with all the same conjugation patterns (делать -> доделать), likewise with "live," which becomes "survive" (жить -> выжить), no extra work required.

With this triage of tools, you can facilitate repetition: jumpstart your brain's recognition process for language and the rest will fall into place.

Of course, it'd be stupid to just mine the dictionary for flashcards to practice. Unless your brain has some *reason* to remember the language, you'll forget it as soon as you learn it. That's where the *meaning* part comes in.

I use *meaningful* in the broadest sense possible here. Whatever makes the language learning process fun or memorable for you is useful. Learning is all about connections: *what* connects is lodged in place through repetition, *why* you connect it depends on you. Know what makes the info stick for you. Here are some ideas to get you started:

- **Children's books:** avoid the ones for infants because they suck (few or sometimes no words). Ones for slightly older kids can be surprisingly good, though. Chances are you can learn about the mythology or traditions of the country in the process too.
- **Children's songs:** these are underrated. Nursery rhymes, lullabies, and mnemonic jingles are an integral part of growing up and continue to influence you as an adult. Learn them and you'll be learning a cornerstone of the language; by that same token, you'll also score brownie points with your students.

- **TV:** the best thing on TV is commercials. Advertising uses simplified, catchy language which can be of great use to you. Don't even worry about specific shows, just flip around until you find something that speaks to you.
- **Subtitles:** you'll get tired of language immersion eventually (don't feel bad about it). At that point, you'll probably revert to whatever media you're most comfortable with. Whether it's a videogame or a movie, though, see if you can set subtitles for it. That media is already meaningful for you, so you can take advantage of it to pick up stray bits of vocabulary and grammar.
- **Hobby groups/community groups:** what's your hobby? (You see how that question always pops up like that?) Use it to your advantage. If you're into rock climbing, join a rock climbing gym and get friendly with the other climbers. Ditto with sports. Even going to the gym to exercise can be a good way of putting yourself out there. Get chatting with likeminded people and you'll not only find speaking partners, you'll find meaningful connections. (I don't do this, hence the following).
- **Italki:** if, like me, you suck at human interactions, then the internet will be your go-to place for speaking partners. There are multiple sites out there where people practice speaking together, but the only one I can recommend from experience is Italki (https://www.italki.com/). It's free and it's got a good user-base. Mention you're a teacher of English and that'll put you head and shoulders above the competition.
- **Don't discount your students as a resource:** (yet another reason why the ENGLISH ONLY policy is stupid). Piggyback on whatever you're teaching your students as an opportunity for you to learn their language. They'll find it flattering, give you feedback in

real time, and you'll build rapport as they laugh at your pitiful attempts at pronouncing their language. This'll even reinforce their own learning in the process.

These are just a few ideas. Start Googling and you'll find a glut of other bullet point lists just like mine from people who profess to have found the secret of language acquisition. If media suggestions are *specifically* what you're looking for, then dive in. Otherwise, don't waste your time because every super-secret learning philosophy out there eventually boils down to meaningful repetition anyway.

Always ask yourself (1) is this meaningful? Will the media that you're consuming lodge in your brain because you like it? Or! Is the experience at least unpleasant enough to sear related language into your memory? Does it contain words or phrases that normal people use in everyday life? Will you have an associated memory—like a story or an image—that you can use to call up the target language?

(2) How can I facilitate repetition of the material? Even if you have the best grammar book in the world, you'll immediately forget the lesson if you don't repeat it somehow. If it's a simple piece of language (say gendered adjectives or the letters, for example), then you'll see it everywhere and be able to file it away in your brain. If it's something important, but not so common (e.g. how to say "as... as..."), then you ought to stimulate some artificial repetition to make it stick—write it on a sticky note, awkwardly shove it into your day-to-day speech—just do *something* because otherwise the language slips out of your brain and you've got no foundation to build upon for future learning.

However you do it, stick to those two tenets, be realistic, and you'll be well on your way to learning.

CONCLUSION

You carry it with you

There are two times I remember having cried in the last decade or two of my life. One was when I fell off my scooter and broke my leg at the age of 12 (I had it coming, honestly; I was a pretty snotty kid) and the other was a few nights before I left Japan.

It snuck up on me. There I was packing my stuff—taking down the dozens of posters and pictures I'd accumulated, folding the clothing I knew I wouldn't need, eating rice straight out of the pot—and then it hit me. I was looking at a Lego Pikachu, a gift from one of my students. Pokemon had become an off-and-on topic for us because her daughter liked it. Nothing too personal, just a small recognition of a brief interaction we'd had. It wasn't even my favorite character or anything.

But it was enough.

In that moment, it was like all the feelings of the year came rushing out of me in one burst. All the doubts and regrets about how much I sucked as a teacher. All the botched classes. The feeling of unworthiness that I felt whenever I got gifts. The awe that alien land I would probably never see again provoked in me. The frustration at having made so little progress in Japanese. It all came out.

I wasn't just crying. I choked. I hacked. I felt like a piece of paper being crumpled up into an ever-smaller and smaller ball.

My body seemed just as confused as I was. I was on autopilot, heating water for my evening coffee, boiling a pot of eggs for next day's lunch as I did every day. I must've made for a hilarious sight: this massive foreigner wearing shorts, a T-shirt, a coat (because it was simultaneously hot and cold in the apartment) and shuffling around in slippers, heavily sobbing in between sips of coffee.

And it didn't stop. After about an hour of surfing the web while still crying, I tried going to sleep and just couldn't. I hadn't had anything substantial for dinner, but still thought it was a good idea to down half a bottle of wine. My stomach was on fire, the alcohol was taking effect, but I still couldn't sleep because of the chronic sobbing. In yet another flash of brilliance, I decided to go for a walk—without my glasses or contacts.

I stumbled blindly through the dark streets, still crying. It must've been past midnight because the roads were empty, stores were closed, and any people I saw were just passing blips in the landscape. I drifted through the commercial district and down to the river. My town was famous for this river—a man-made one. The daimyo of our region had built it for his wife when she, taken from the comfort of her native Kyoto, felt homesick for the beauty of nature and temples she knew there. Gives a whole new meaning to the phrase "cry me a river," huh?

I sat on the bank of the river for a while, still feeling like hell, and the moment passed.

If you skipped to the end of this book looking for an answer to the question "should I do it?" (and no judgments here if you did —I do the same thing sometimes) then (1) you missed the point of the book, and (2) the answer is *yes*.

Call me a hypocrite, but I didn't re-up for Japan. As I said before, teaching is a means to an end for me. I entered it with the vague objective of completing myself—ostensibly as an anthropologist, a language learner, but more honestly as a person.

I wouldn't be who I am today without the experiences I had as a teacher. It strained me in precisely the ways I hoped it would. I was broken out of my shell and forced to be sociable, independent, composed, sympathetic, enthusiastic—insert any other positive job application word you can think of there, I had it.

I carry that with me.

I wanna recommend you a movie. It's called *Paris, I Love You*. It's made up of different vignettes, all taking place in the city and connected to the heart of whatever "Paris" is. Amidst stories of vampires, gay sculptors, divorcees, Muslims, and taxi drivers, there's this one piece about a postal worker from Denver who visits the city on vacation. She speaks French well, but does so in a hysterically bad accent that makes you think "are you even trying?" It's all narrated in her voice as she totters about visiting the essential tourist sites and trying to interact with the locals. Like her accent, her character just doesn't match up with the glamor of the city. For every monumental place she visits, the only commentary she can offer is banalities about a past boyfriend and her dogs.

There's a moment, though, which transcends all of that. She sits down for lunch in a non-descript park, surrounded by Parisians going about their everyday life, starts munching on a massive sandwich, and then it happens. What *it* is even she can't describe. She's overcome by a feeling of deep emotion, a joy and sadness "like remembering something she'd never known before or had always been waiting for," in her words. The only conclusion she can draw is "I felt alive."

www.ingramcontent.com/pod-product-compliance
Lightning Source LLC
Chambersburg PA
CBHW072045280526
45788CB00006B/2189